English Concept Cartoons®

Written by

Jane Turner, Chris Smith, Brenda Keogh and Stuart Naylor.

*For Mum –
my degree wasn't
a total
waste.

Love

Jane
x*

Millgate House Education

First published in 2014 by Millgate House Publishers

Millgate House Publishers is an imprint of
Millgate House Education Ltd.
Unit 1, Zan Business Park
Crewe Road
Sandbach
Cheshire
CW11 4QD
UK

www.millgatehouse.co.uk

Copyright © Millgate House Education 2014

British Library Cataloguing in Publication Data
A catalogue record for this book is available from the British Library.

ISBN 978-0-9562646-6-4

Graphic design by Bill Corrigan & Neil Pepper
Illustrations by Ged Mitchell

Printed and bound in Great Britain by MWL Print Group

Contents

i. Acknowledgements

This book (and CD ROM) follows its partner publications, Concept Cartoons in Science Education (Naylor, S. and Keogh, B. 2000) and Concept Cartoons in Mathematics Education (Dabell, J., Keogh, B. and Naylor, S. 2008). We have used a broadly similar format for the Concept Cartoons and the background text, so that readers who are familiar with the science or mathematics Concept Cartoons will feel at home with these examples in English.

Our thanks go to:

- Illustrator Ged Mitchell, whose drawings bring our ideas to life

- Project manager Jo Williams, whose questions, comments and ideas have been so useful

- Graphic designers Bill Corrigan and Neil Pepper for patiently turning ideas into a reality

- Colleagues, teachers and learners of all ages, particularly those at Iver School, who have provided the inspiration for many of the Concept Cartoons

- Teachers and advisors in Buckinghamshire, Luton and Edinburgh who have provided invaluable help in developing and trialling the Concept Cartoons

- Elizabeth Smith, Grant Bage and Chris Collins who helped at every stage from inspiration to editing, and have added great insight to the Concept Cartoons.

ii. Essential Information

Each Concept Cartoon has support material, with ideas for follow up activities and background information together with extension ideas.

Concept Cartoons are normally used near the start of a lesson, followed by paired or small group discussion, and then an opportunity to explore or research the ideas being discussed. You do not need long periods of discussion to have an impact on the lesson.

Ask learners to discuss why each character in the Concept Cartoon might hold their particular idea. What might go in the blank speech bubble?

Some Concept Cartoons might initially appear too easy for some learners, but they can provide a useful starting point for discussion about more complex ideas and often reveal some basic misunderstandings. They can also be used with learners who lack confidence or experience in English. **If you have the CD ROM you can adjust the level of demand by changing the text.**

Avoid being judgemental when learners are sharing their ideas, as this will close down debate and minimise the development of new ideas and understanding. The uncertainty created by the Concept Cartoons is productive.

The main body of a lesson should provide an opportunity for learners to explore, challenge or consolidate the ideas raised through the Concept Cartoon(s). Allow time at the end of the lesson for learners to share their ideas and opinions. Have they changed their minds and why? Do they want to add any new ideas to the Concept Cartoon?

Learners can create their own Concept Cartoons as a way of assessing and reviewing their current skills and knowledge in English.

If you want to know more about Concept Cartoons and how they are used, please visit:

www.millgatehouse.co.uk

The Concept Cartoons in this book are also available on an interactive CD ROM. More information about using the CD ROM can be found on the following page.

English Concept Cartoons CD ROM

(this is available separately)

The CD ROM contains all the Concept Cartoons plus suggestions for follow up activities and background information together with extension ideas.

The speech bubbles on the CD ROM and some of the text in the central images are fully writable. **Remember to print out any new Concept Cartoons that you create.**

Using the features on the CD ROM

The writable speech bubbles allow you to:

- change what the characters are saying
- add learners' ideas to those in the Concept Cartoons
- keep a printed record of learners' ideas
- create new Concept Cartoons
- encourage learners to create their own Concept Cartoons for other groups.

The writable central images allow you to:

- change the nature or context of the Concept Cartoon
- increase the level of demand of the Concept Cartoon
- create more Concept Cartoons around the same basic idea.

The follow up activities allow you to:

- encourage learners to think about why the characters hold the alternative ideas
- provide more challenges related to the concept being explored
- encourage some learners to work more independently.

The background ideas enable you to:

- share possible ways to solve the problem with your learners
- provide more challenges related to the concept being explored
- encourage some learners to work more independently.

Any Concept Cartoons created by using this software are for use by the purchasing organisation only and must not be given, or sold, to other individuals or organisations without prior permission from Millgate House Education.

iii. Background Information

What are Concept Cartoons?

'Concept Cartoons are cartoon-style
drawings that put forward a
range of viewpoints about speaking,
reading and writing English in everyday situations.'

They are designed to intrigue, to provoke discussion and to stimulate thinking. By offering different opinions about English conventions and stylistic devices and their effects, Concept Cartoons open discussion and provide a stimulus for developing ideas and skills further. They do not always have a single right answer as there is frequently an element of subjectivity or personal choice involved. Judgements may depend on a number of different things, including contextual factors, intended impact or the constraints of grammar, spelling or convention. We believe that Concept Cartoons are a unique approach to teaching, learning and assessment in English.

Research into Concept Cartoons in Science (Keogh and Naylor, 1999) identifies a number of features that help to make Concept Cartoons effective. These include:

· visual representation of ideas

· minimal text, in dialogue form

· using familiar situations

· offering alternative viewpoints, including the correct or most acceptable ideas

· common areas of misunderstanding, drawn from research and professional practice

· giving the alternatives equal status.

How are Concept Cartoons used?

Concept Cartoons are used in a variety of ways and in a wide range of settings. The most common reasons for using them are:

· making the learners' ideas explicit
· challenging and developing the learners' ideas
· illustrating alternative viewpoints
· providing a stimulus for discussion and argument
· promoting thinking and reasoning
· helping learners to ask their own questions
· providing starting points for learners' own speaking, reading and writing
· raising awareness of how and why a writer has constructed a text and what influences a reader's response
· creating a sense of purpose for the rest of the lesson
· promoting involvement and enhancing motivation
· posing open-ended questions
· as extension or consolidation activities
· as a summary of a topic or revision
· outside lesson time (e.g. homework).

**'Concept Cartoons are often used at the start of a lesson
or topic as a stimulus for discussion, to identify areas of
uncertainty and to suggest questions to be answered.'**

Concept Cartoons are generally used to start a lesson or topic, but they can be used part-way through, or at the end, where the emphasis is on consolidating learning in a new situation. A short period of individual reflection on a Concept Cartoon before discussion starts can be useful for clarifying ideas; similarly some individual follow up after discussion and/or research can be useful for consolidating learning.

**'Teachers and student teachers also use Concept Cartoons
for developing their own subject knowledge, by asking questions
that they may not have thought of asking themselves.'**

Teachers and student teachers can use English Concept Cartoons to develop both an awareness of mistakes that learners commonly make, and an understanding of the impact of personal experience and preference in a response to reading a text or completing a writing task. They reinforce the idea of English as a living language. Speakers and writers are constantly making choices about how to use, and sometimes abuse, the rules and conventions of English to communicate their message most effectively. Listeners and readers also make choices, sometimes conscious, sometimes not, about how they interpret and understand the message. English Concept Cartoons puts the awareness that speech and texts are purposefully created at the heart of English teaching and learning.

8

The writable bubbles allow learners to add ideas and to include the mistakes that they think other people might make. Learners can create their own Concept Cartoons to illustrate possible areas of confusion or disagreement in a topic. Teachers can create their own Concept Cartoons to change the level of demand, or explore different words in the same situation.

Concept Cartoons and Talk

Several features of Concept Cartoons help to promote talk between learners:

- the visual stimulus that puts the text in a context, making the literacy theme or grammatical rule accessible and meaningful

- the limited amount of text, which makes them especially suitable for learners with poor literacy (reading) skills

- the cartoon-style format and everyday settings give a strong message of familiarity, making the situations seem accessible

- presenting ideas in deceptively simple situations promotes engagement with those ideas

- the dialogue between the characters seems to draw learners into their conversation, almost as though the learners are participating in their debate.

The value of encouraging learners to talk and argue about their ideas is widely recognised in schools. Teachers may have some concerns about managing this interaction, but using Concept Cartoons enables talk and argument to take place in a controlled and purposeful way. Concept Cartoons provide a focus, context and a purpose for discussion, and they legitimise argument between learners. This kind of talk supports learning (Alexander, 2006). Having to justify one's ideas to other learners in the group is a powerful mechanism for developing deeper understanding.

9

> 'Using Concept Cartoons helps learners who lack
> confidence to share their ideas.'

Having different characters putting forward the various alternatives and opinions helps to raise the status of each of the alternatives. The threat to a learner's self-esteem from putting forward incorrect ideas is therefore reduced. Having voices speaking for them helps to engage learners who may be reluctant to put forward their own ideas in case they are wrong. It also gives learners the confidence to value their own ideas, especially in circumstances where there is no single correct answer and their subjective opinion can be valid if well-justified.

Concept Cartoons and Learning

> 'The potential of generating cognitive conflict means that Concept
> Cartoons can be useful for all learners of English, regardless of their
> skills and experience.'

All of the alternatives in each of the Concept Cartoons are of equal status. There are no contextual clues, such as facial expressions or one character always having the best understanding, so all learners are likely to experience cognitive conflict and find that their ideas are challenged. Engagement with a Concept Cartoon can lead to a clarification of ideas, more secure learning and translation of knowledge into deeper understanding. One useful approach is to invite learners to work out why each of the characters might think their idea is correct.

Using Concept Cartoons has implications for the role of teachers and learners in the classroom. In most classrooms, learners put forward ideas and the teacher evaluates them. However with Concept Cartoons, alternative ideas are presented to the learners and they adjudicate between them themselves. This is a fairly fundamental shift in role.

> 'Even though the teacher has the overall responsibility for managing
> learning, Concept Cartoons give learners more responsibility
> in the process and the value of their active involvement is enhanced.'

One very significant aspect of Concept Cartoons is motivation. As teachers we know that motivated learners are more effective learners, and that if learners are disaffected or alienated then there is often little real learning taking place. In our experience, teachers using Concept Cartoons consistently find that their learners are more motivated and engaged.

10

Concept Cartoons, Assessment and Learning

> 'Concept Cartoons help to put the principles of
> assessment for learning into practice.'

Concept Cartoons can be used for individual summative assessment. However they are probably more valuable as an assessment for learning tool, in which assessment is used to make learning more effective (Black and Wiliam, 1998; Black et al, 2002; Marshall and Wiliam, 2006, Wiliam 2011). As learners make their ideas public, the teacher is able to make informal judgements about their ideas, and the reasons behind them. It quickly becomes apparent whether learners have a good grasp of the grammatical rules or literary conventions involved, are struggling to make sense of the situation or have firmly held preference or ideas which are influencing their thinking. The teacher can then take these ideas into account as the lesson progresses.

Meanwhile learners have the opportunity to discuss their ideas and to become more aware of what they and their peers think. Concept Cartoons encourage vigorous discussion and debate, and sometimes this can be enough to change a learner's idea or broaden their understanding. More frequently, the discussion raises the need for further investigation or research, perhaps looking for more examples or considering how the idea would work in a different context. In this way using Concept Cartoons for assessment provides a starting point for learning and helps learners create their own learning agenda.

> 'Concept Cartoons identify what learners understand, and create the need
> for further enquiry and learning to resolve the conflict between ideas.'

We have used the term 'Active Assessment' to describe this connection, in which purposeful, thought-provoking assessment activities become an integral part of the learning process (Keogh, Dabell and Naylor 2008). Concept Cartoons are not the only active learning approach to assessment. Wiliam (2011) also gives excellent descriptions of a range of techniques that can be used in a similar way. However Concept Cartoons are particularly effective at getting learners thinking about their own ideas and how they might need to develop or broaden. They promote metacognition – in other words they help learners to think about their own learning. Even quite young children have commented on how Concept Cartoons make them think about their own ideas and those of other people.

11

> 'The realisation that there can be lots of ways of thinking about a piece of text or speech can be a powerful incentive to taking other people's ideas seriously.'

Getting learners to create Concept Cartoons for their peers or for younger learners is a good way of assessing their current understanding. They will need to think of possible alternatives as well as ensuring that they have included the acceptable English usage.

When Concept Cartoons were first generated, it was thought they would need to be targeted at particular ages. Experience has shown that this is not necessarily true, and that many of the Concept Cartoons can be suitable for a very wide age range.

> 'Learners can often tackle a Concept Cartoon at their own level of understanding or experience, and will interpret the problems raised in different ways according to their own individual starting points.'

The same Concept Cartoon may be used on more than one occasion and still provide a suitable level of challenge. The blank speech bubbles, and writable central features of the CD ROM, add to the scope of many of the Concept Cartoons.

Language variation

1

I

Language variation

1.1 Living language

Talk to people who were born a long time ago and compare the words that you and they use. You can also look at new story books and those written a long time ago. See if you can find examples of words whose meanings have changed over time. Are there examples of words that have been created recently or words that we don't use any more? If so, why do you think these changes have taken place? Create a display of new and old words and any words that you find that have changed their meaning.

Many things cause language to change over time, such as how people live, where they travel to and from, new technology and young people trying to be different from adults. Words can change in different ways. For example, a word can take a more general or a more specific meaning – *place* used to mean a broad street and *deer* used to mean a wild animal of any kind. Some words can take a more or less pleasant meaning – *crafty* used to mean strong and *queen* used to mean woman. Did you find any other examples? Why do we need to invent new words? Imagine you are writing a new edition of a dictionary. How will you decide which new words to add and which words to take out? Create some new entries for the dictionary.

Language variation

1.2 Origin of words

Find out how café became part of our language and where it came from. You may need to use books and the internet to help you. Is the same word used in any other countries? Do any countries have their own word? Do we have any other words to describe a café? If not, why not? Now try to invent a word of your own for café.

Café means coffee in French. Café was first used in English to describe a coffee house. We now use the word more generally to mean a place where you sit at a table to have a drink and something light to eat. Some people use the slang word *caff* instead of café. It is possible that the word has its origins in the Arabic word *qahwa*. Many countries use a similar word for coffee, such as the Turkish word *kahve* and the Italian word *caffe*. English uses words from many other languages, such as French and Latin. Think about words for food. How do you think these words became part of English everyday language? Can you find some words that have moved from English to other languages? Do you think every language should have their own words, or is it OK to use the same words across different languages? Why do you think that? Does everyone have the same view?

1.3 What is a language?

Find out all you can about Esperanto. Where did it come from? Who speaks it and can everybody understand it? Do people use it in their everyday lives? How does it compare with other languages? Share your ideas about Esperanto and other languages with another group. Why do you think we need to invent a new language when we already have lots of different languages already? Do you all agree?

Esperanto was created in the 1880s. Esperanto means 'one who hopes'. It was created as a language that would be easy to learn and enable people around the globe to communicate with each other in one common language. Although some people argue that it is not a real language, it is spoken by people living in many countries. It has many of the features of other languages such as grammar, vocabulary, new words being introduced, and so on. It is said to be a good basic language to learn in preparation for learning other languages. How does Esperanto compare with other made-up languages, such as Na'vi as spoken in the film Avatar, or the language spoken by the Klingons in the television programme Star Trek? If you want to create a new language, what would you need to think about? Think about all the languages spoken in your class as a starting point.

Language variation

1.4 Dialect

Find out what is meant by 'standard English' and what is meant by 'local dialect'. Do you have a dialect? How do you know it's a dialect? Try to interview or find a recording of someone speaking in a strong local dialect. How easy are they to understand? Does it matter if you can't understand them? When do people use a dialect and when do they use standard English? How do they decide which to use? Is a dialect used in writing or only in speaking? Young people often use words that adults don't. Does that mean they have their own dialect?

The words *yer* (you're) *reet* (right) and *nesh* (over-sensitive) are used in Lancashire, as in "What do you mean, it's cold? Yer reet nesh, you are." These words are part of the local dialect rather than standard English. Areas of many countries have a local dialect, with specific words and phrases that visitors may not understand. Dialects are part of a language, but there is not a sharp distinction between a dialect and a language. Split into groups to carry out more research into different dialects. Why do you think different regions develop different dialects? Some dialects are dying out. Why do you think that might be happening? Is this a good or bad thing for the language?

1.5 Regional variations

Do people sometimes use different words for the same thing? Why does this happen? Does it matter if there are two words for the same thing? What about more than two? Find out how many different words there are for a bread roll. Were you surprised by what you discovered? Find as many examples as you can of regional variations for everyday words.

Regional differences in the way language has developed mean that people use different words for the same thing. They also use variations in grammar and pronunciation. Some people think that some regional forms of language are of lower social status than others. This means that language can change as some people try to lose a regional accent and avoid using the words that are commonly used in their part of the country. Sometimes words used in certain parts of the country become fashionable, so people in other parts of the country start to build them into their own vocabulary too (*innit*, for example). Find as many examples as you can of this happening. Someone who moves to a different part of the country might change the words they use to the local variation. Why do you think they might do this?

1.6 Symbols in language

How many emoticons can you find? Talk about which ones you know and where they are used. Why do people use them? Do emoticons only express feelings? Are they better than words? Would they be used in a business email? What do the answers to these questions tell you about whether emoticons are becoming part of our language? Write a message using as many emoticons as possible, and then write one using words to replace the emoticons. How easy is it to do this? Which message do others prefer and why?

Emoticons are icons used to express emotions in messages. The word emoticon is made up from the English words emotion and icon. In emails and texts they are made from punctuation marks, numbers and letters to create faces that display emotions. They can be useful in short messages, where someone can convey an emotion without having to write a word, phrase or sentence. People think that they are a modern creation but something similar to emoticons first appeared in the late 1800s. These written symbols are now becoming part of the written language in many countries. There are dictionaries of emoticons on the internet. Are different emoticons used in different countries? Find other examples where symbols are used instead of words. When are they helpful? Is it possible to make a whole language from symbols?

1.7 Numbers or words

Look at different places where writing is used such as comics, books, packaging, adverts and texts. When and why do people use numerals in their writing? Where can you find numerals being used instead of letters and words, for example *8* instead of *ate*? Is there a difference between the way large and small numbers are written? Do you agree with the way words and numerals are used? Does this make writing easier or harder to understand?

Words and numbers are part of language. How they are used in writing depends on what you are writing and your audience. The biggest recent change in using numerals in written language is where words or parts of words are replaced by them, such as *4* instead of *for*. This is done most commonly in texts and emails, and not normally in more formal writing or where information needs to be very clear. If you are writing a number, you need to decide whether to use a numeral or a word to represent it. Usually numbers up to ten are spelled out rather than using numerals. Some people spell out one-word numbers, e.g. *twelve*, but write two-word numbers as numerals, e.g. *54*. Create a guide for younger children for how to use numerals in their writing.

1.8 Sport talk

Watch a short video of people playing tennis, and listen to the commentary and the words the umpire uses. Which words have a special meaning? Try to find out where the words have come from. How are these words written? Are any of the words used in everyday language? Find out about words used in other sports. Are any of the same words used in more than one sport? Some sporting phrases have become part of everyday language, for example out for the count. Try to find some more of these. Create a dictionary of special sporting words and phrases.

There are many special words used in sport and everyday words that have a different meaning. Some are derived from foreign words, for example *love* in tennis comes from the French word, *l'oeuf* meaning egg. This is because the shape of an egg is like the figure zero. Some special words are made up, and some come from songs, slang, names of people and words that were around at the time the sport was developing. Sometimes the words in sport change their meaning, just as words do in everyday language. For example, *try* in rugby originally meant to kick for goal. Invent a new game with its own special language. What words will you use? Try to use words from different sources.

Language variation

Speaking and listening

2

2

Speaking and listening

2.1 What is communication?

Find out about different ways of communicating. How many different types of communication can you find? Can it be communication if it does not use words? Think about how we give information to other people. Does this change depending on who we are communicating with or what we are communicating? If you receive information, but do not understand it (it might be in a foreign language or a strong regional accent, for example), has communication taken place?

Communication can include words, pictures, signs and movements. Communication needs a sender, a message, and a receiver who understands the message. Often we communicate by speaking. People who understand sign language can use that to communicate. Communication can be written, such as using a poster, a text, a letter, a powerpoint presentation, an email or a message on an internet social network. You can also communicate using non-verbal communication such as body language, facial expressions and gestures. Often we combine different kinds of communication to share ideas and information. Think of some different scenarios such as teaching an idea to younger children, getting an urgent message to someone or communicating with someone at a noisy rock concert. How do you decide which forms of communication to use? How do you make sure that your information is understood? Does everyone agree with your ideas?

2.2 Is texting a conversation?

Think about what is meant by the word 'conversation' and talk with a friend about whether you are having a conversation when you text each other. How many text messages would it need to make a conversation? Or can it never be called a conversation? If one person asks a question and the other person answers yes or no, would that be a conversation? Are there fewer or more questions involved in a text message than a spoken conversation? Why do you think this is?

A conversation needs to be interactive but it does not always need to involve speaking, so texting can be called a conversation. Text conversations often have a different format from spoken conversations. Having a text conversation is quick and concise, and sometimes this can be an advantage. In other circumstances it may be a disadvantage. For example, think about the emotions involved in a conversation – it may make you happy, sad, angry, confused, upset. How you respond, how you convey your feelings and how you manage your feelings will be different if you are speaking to somebody rather than texting them. Conversations by text appear to be increasing and conversations by phone are declining. Is that a good thing? Think of some different issues that you might want to have a conversation about. Which ones would be best by text, and which would be better by phone or face to face? Why do you think that? Does everyone agree?

2.3 Regional accents

Listen to people talking with different accents. Can you recognise where the accent comes from? Are people easy to understand when they talk in regional accents? Does everyone with a particular accent also use a regional dialect? See if you can find a recording of an early TV or radio broadcast. What are the differences between how presenters spoke then and how they speak now? Is there such a thing as not having an accent?

In the first television and radio broadcasts the presenters used a style of English known as received pronunciation. Noticeable regional accents were not considered suitable. Why do you think that was? However, received pronunciation is also considered to be an accent associated with particular social groups and with connections to parts of southern England. Nowadays more people who broadcast to the public have noticeable regional accents. Call centres are often located in certain parts of the country because it is believed that listeners prefer particular accents and consider them to be trustworthy. What do you think about this? What are the positive and negative impacts of hearing a wider range of accents? Even though regional accents are more accepted, some people still try to lose their accents if they want to work in certain professions. Do you think that they should do this? Why? Do you all agree?

Speaking and listening

2.4 Discussion

Take it in turn to listen to people in your group having a discussion and watch how they interact. Think about what everyone did and how that helped the discussion. Is listening important in a discussion? Does everyone need to take turns? If only one person speaks, is this a discussion? Can you have a discussion with yourself? Is it possible to be involved in more than one discussion at a time? Try it and see what happens.

A discussion is a way of sharing ideas, thoughts and information. Discussions are interactive, so people involved in discussions should try to respond to each other's ideas. In some discussions you might decide to take turns to make sure everyone's ideas are heard. Sometimes what one person says will overlap with what someone else is saying. This is normal and is how ideas develop. It is important to try to share your ideas in a discussion, but you also need to make sure that you do not talk so much that other people's ideas cannot be heard. How you decide when to speak may depend on what you know and what you think. Choose a topic to discuss and record your discussion. What could you have done to improve your discussion? Think about your own role and that of others. Would using questions help? Do any rules help? What is the best way to make sure that everyone who wants to speak is heard, without spoiling the flow of the discussion?

2.5 Working in a group

Think about when you worked in a group to complete different tasks and how you organised what you did. Which ways work best? Do you always need a leader? How do you decide who does what? Is there ever a time when one person's ideas are more important than the others? Do you need rules to help you to work well? What is the first thing you should do when starting to work together to carry out a task? Why do you think this?

When working on a group task, it is important to make sure that you listen to each other, share ideas and keep everyone actively involved. This means taking enough time at the beginning of the task to share ideas and decide who will do what. The teacher might give you roles. Alternatively, a group leader might help to do this, but their ideas are not any more important than the rest of the group. You might find it useful to stop part way through to talk about how things are going. Sometimes it is helpful to create a small number of rules for how to work. These might include how you will decide what to do if you don't all agree. Think of two rules that you think will make sure your group works well together and finishes the task in time. Which do you think is the most important rule? Does everyone agree?

2.6 Giving a powerpoint presentation

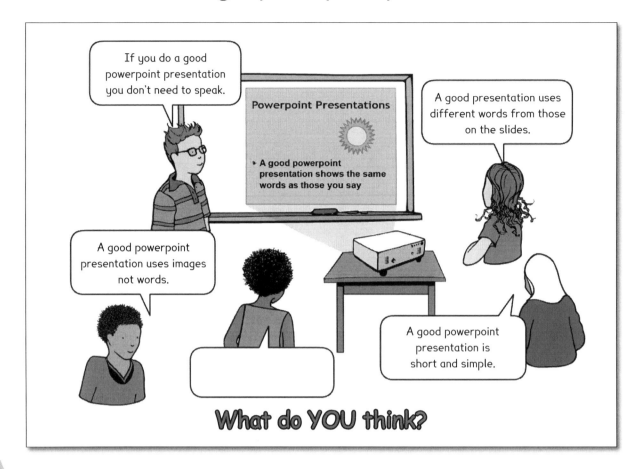

Have a look at some powerpoint presentations. Decide which are the best and worst powerpoint presentations you have seen. Why did you enjoy some but not others? What helps to make them interesting? What doesn't help? It has been suggested that a powerpoint presentation should have no more than ten slides, last no more than twenty minutes and contain no font smaller than thirty point. What do you think about this suggestion? Does a good powerpoint presentation always have animation and sound?

Powerpoints can be very complicated and include videos, music and animations, or they can be very simple. Making a very complicated powerpoint is not always the best way to share ideas. Usually clear and simple is more effective. How you use the powerpoint is important. It is not very interesting if each slide has too much information on it, or there are so many slides that you have to go through them too quickly. It is boring if you simply read what is on the slide. Thinking about what kinds of presentation you prefer will help you to prepare a good presentation that interests other people. What difference does it make if you are presenting alone or in a group? When would you choose a powerpoint presentation to communicate ideas, and when would another way of presenting be better? What would influence your choice?

2.7 Is it OK to shout?

Think about when you shout and why. Can you think of a situation when it is really important that you shout? Can you think of times when you really shouldn't shout? Talk about these situations and explain to others in your group why you chose them. What do they think? Does the number of people you are talking to make a difference to how you speak? Should you let your emotions decide how you will speak? Think about times when you are very angry, happy or upset. Is it always possible to control how you speak?

You can change the volume of your voice a lot. From the sound of your voice, your listeners will make judgments about what you are saying and your attitude towards them. Shouting might make people think that you are angry when you are not angry. If you shout all the time, people might not listen to what you have to say. Shouting will have most impact if you don't usually shout. Shouting may change the vocabulary you use. You may well find that your sentences are shorter and your vocabulary is simpler when you shout. Why do you think this is? Create some scenarios and act them out with your group in different ways, changing the volume and tone of the voices you use. Then discuss the impact of these different voices.

31

2.8 Use of language

Talk with your group about times when you were angry with someone. What did you say and how did you say it? Why does the character think you shouldn't say 'Shut your face' to an adult? Do you think this means that it is alright to say it to a child? Is there a difference between speaking to a child and an adult? If someone is rude to you, does that give you the right to be rude to them? Being angry may change how you speak, but does that make it right to be rude? Which is more important – what you say or how you say it?

There are many ways of expressing how you feel, and you need to choose the way that will help you make your point clearly. If you upset someone by being rude, they are less likely to understand your viewpoint. You are therefore less likely to get what you want. In school there are often different rules for how you speak to adults and how you speak to your peers. Some people say swearing and being rude show that you are uneducated and if you had a better vocabulary, you wouldn't need to do this. Do you agree? Talk about this with your group.

2.9 Figuratively speaking

Collect some figures of speech that you or your friends use. Do you agree about what they mean? Why do people choose to use figures of speech instead of saying what they mean? How do you decide if they are speaking literally or figuratively? Is there only one meaning for each figure of speech, or do they sometimes have more than one meaning? If someone uses a figure of speech, does it change the way you react to what they say? Find some figures of speech that you have never heard of before. Work out what they mean with the rest of your group.

Figurative language is the opposite of literal. Literal language says things exactly as they are – *he ran fast*, for example. Figurative language paints a picture for the reader or listener that gives a clearer or more detailed image. For example, you are using figurative language if you use the simile, *he ran like the wind. Pull your socks up* is an example of an idiom. The adult doesn't really want the child to do anything with their socks. It's just a figure of speech. Hyperbole is also a figure of speech that uses an exaggerated or extravagant statement. For example, *I will die if she asks me to dance*. It is important that the listener is not confused by the figure of speech that you use. Have a go at creating your own figures of speech and try them out on each other.

2.10 Rhetorical questions

What do you think rhetorical means? If somebody said *Do you think I was born yesterday?* to you, would you understand what they meant or would you be confused? A question usually means someone wants an answer. How do you think this teacher might respond if the pupil answered 'No'? Is there any point in asking a rhetorical question if someone has never heard of it before? Find some more examples of rhetorical questions and discuss when they might be used.

A rhetorical question is a figure of speech in the form of a question that is used for effect. The person using it is not expecting an answer, and they don't expect the question to be taken literally. The answer may be obvious, or the questioner might immediately give the answer themselves. Sometimes it can seem offensive if the listener responds as though it is a literal question. Some examples of rhetorical questions are:

· *Can't you do anything right?*
· *Do bears live in woods?*
· *Are you pulling my leg?*

See if you can find some rhetorical questions in a piece of text and discuss why you think they might be used. Try conversations using rhetorical questions in your group. How do you think people are likely to respond to them?

34

Books and the art of writing

3

3

Books and the art of writing

3.1 Being a writer

Think about a favourite object or place. Write about it in three different ways – a poem, a story and a report. Look at what you have written. Does what you write depend on the kind of writing you are doing? Would the writing be different if you had written about something else? Does this matter? Compare your work with others in your class. How is it the same and how is it different? How does what you write change depending on who you are writing for?

When you are writing you can experiment with using different words and styles. It is good to use new ways of writing and even to make up your own words at times. However, the audience is likely to make a difference to what and how you write. This means that you need to think carefully about the choice of words and the style you use. The purpose of the writing usually has an impact on the vocabulary you use. A poem is likely to contain more similes and metaphors than a report. Some people think that the more you read, the better you write. How can reading help you become a better writer? Choose a subject, for example *Monday morning*. Try writing about it using different genres and styles. How much can you vary your style? What do others think about your writing?

3.2 Writer's block

Talk to each other about when you found it really difficult to write. Do you all agree about what makes a difference? Ask your partner to choose a subject for your writing. Set a word limit, for example two hundred words. Write about it in a set amount of time without using a dictionary. Does not knowing how to spell some words, or having a time and word limit, make a difference to how well you write? Would it have been easier to choose your own subject? How do you come up with the ideas for what to write? What do others in your group think?

All writers are different. What is easy for some writers is difficult for others. Some writers find spelling difficult. Often they will write down their ideas first and check the spelling later, rather than losing the flow of their writing. Some find looking through a dictionary or a thesaurus gives them ideas. Some writers take a break if they can't think what to write. Research is helpful for writing non-fiction, as well as some types of fiction such as crime or historical novels. People might think of a character in a book and imagine them in a different story. Some writers think about something that has happened to themselves or a friend. What other ways can you think of that help you to write? Make a list of everyone's ideas and try some for yourself. Which ones do you think are the most useful?

3.3 Redrafting writing

Think about when you redrafted your own writing. How does redrafting help? Does it involve adding things or removing things, or both? Does it ever involve changing characters? Does it help to stop part way through and re-read what has been written, or is it better to keep writing to the end and then re-read? Are there any times when redrafting doesn't help to improve writing? Try redrafting a piece of writing as soon as you have finished it, the next day and a week later. How much do you change each time? Why do you think this is? How do you decide when the writing is finished?

Redrafting writing should make it better – for example, fuller, more interesting, clearer or more accurate. You might improve a story by using more senses to describe the setting, or giving the characters more expressions, or varying the length of the sentences in your story. You might change the way a poem flows or the rhymes you use. You might clarify some information in factual writing. You might identify better ways to structure your sentences and paragraphs, or spot words that are not spelt correctly. Even though it will take some time to redraft writing, it is usually time well spent. Take a story or a piece of factual writing that someone else has written. See if you can improve the writing by redrafting it. Share both versions with your partner. Do they think you have improved the writing?

3.4 Using a thesaurus

What do YOU think?

Write a sentence with the word *nice* in it. Then look up *nice* in a thesaurus. Do you understand all the words suggested? Try each of the suggested words in its place. Do they all make sense? If any of the words don't make sense, try to change your sentence so that the words fit better. Are any of the words better than *nice*? If you are not allowed to use the word *nice*, which of the other words would you choose and why?

Some words do not tell us much about the thing being described. For example, if you write *It was a nice day*, what does that tell the reader about the day? The synonyms in a thesaurus can help you to be more precise or more descriptive. Sometimes it isn't easy to decide if any of the words in the thesaurus are better than the one you first thought of. It may help to try some of the different words, see what they look like in your writing, and then make a decision. Words can have subtly different meanings. You might want to use a dictionary as well as a thesaurus, so you can check whether the word you first thought of is the right word to use. Find a short piece of writing and try replacing some of the words using a thesaurus. How does it change the writing? Is a thesaurus always helpful? What advice would you give someone for using a thesaurus?

Books and the art of writing

3.5 Understanding unfamiliar words

Think about times when you come across unfamiliar words in a book. What strategy do you use when you come across a word that you don't know? Ask your friends what they do. What does your teacher or other people do? Look at a piece of writing you haven't read before. Your teacher might suggest one. Read it on your own and decide what to do about the words that you don't know. Share your ideas. How do you decide what is the best thing to do? How many different strategies are used?

It can be frustrating when you come across a word you don't understand, but it happens to everyone. It is one way of learning new words. Sometimes you can work out what it means by thinking about what the sentence is trying to say, or by looking for other clues. Perhaps it looks like another word you know. Or you might try reading on to see whether you understand what happens next. If you can't work it out, then it helps to look the word up or get someone to explain what it means. If you find out what it means and then read the sentence again to check the meaning in context, it is more likely that you will remember and be able to use the word yourself. What other ways can you use to expand your vocabulary (such as having a word of the day or putting new words you meet in a word bank)?

41

3.6 Looking for bias

Who do you think should be interviewed? Is there anybody else who could be interviewed? Think about why local residents might give a biased opinion of the teenagers. Would they only think about that incident or would they think about previous incidents? What are the different ways in which bias could occur in this report? How could the reporter gain a fairer picture of the situation? Try writing an article about your favourite sports team or celebrity without being biased. Is it difficult to do? Share it with your group. Do they agree that it is unbiased?

Bias is an issue in reporting the news, because any reporting rarely includes all of the facts about a situation. The main prejudice in this situation could be against groups of teenagers. The prejudice might be that of the reporter, or of one, some or all of the people being interviewed. Bias can occur in other kinds of writing too. Bias can occur if the person writing is prejudiced for or against a particular person, group or idea, or if they can't empathise with the person or group they are writing about. What other prejudices could affect the way in which someone writes? Create a list of strategies for how to avoid bias in your writing.

3.7 Accurate information

Think of all the different ways you know of finding information. Think of what sort of information you would look for in each of the sources. Can you be sure that it is accurate? How will you know? How will you know if it is up-to-date? If you research some scientific information (about diet, for example), how do you know whether the facts are up-to-date or accurate? Why might some information be wrong? Try looking up the same piece of information from different sources. Do you get different answers? Why do you think this might be?

There are many different sources of information and you need to be sure that the information you find is accurate. Information changes rapidly, especially with developing news stories, so it might be out of date. Sometimes the person writing the information does not understand it very well themselves. It is important to look at more than one source if you can. You also need to check when it was written and who it was written by. This can make a big difference to how much you can trust the source of information. If information differs, how will you decide what to use? Research and write a short report on a current news story, and challenge your partner to check the accuracy of your information.

3.8 A sense of audience

Look at some writing about different subjects. Compare the words that are used in each one. Is some writing easier to understand than others? Why do you think this is? Are all the books written for the same audience? When might it be helpful to write in formal English? See if you can find some examples of where writers use informal language effectively. Why does it work so well? Try writing a short paragraph about the same thing using formal and informal language. Share it with other groups to see what they think.

It is important to use the appropriate type of vocabulary and style for your audience. Of course this can be a problem if you have never met the person who will be reading your writing. If lots of people will read your work, making sure that your writing is appropriate for all of them can be very difficult. The age of your readers, how many of them there are, what they are interested in and what they already know will make a difference to what you write. Words specific to a subject are called technical vocabulary. Choose a topic that uses technical vocabulary, then write two paragraphs with the same information for different readers and change the text to suit each audience. Talk about how you make them different, why you make these decisions and whether they are effective.

Collins

DEVELOPED FOR THE NEW 2014 CURRICULUM

SNAP SCIENCE

THE NEW DYNAMIC TOOLKIT WITH EVERYTHING YOU NEED TO GET YOUR TEETH INTO PRIMARY SCIENCE

WRITTEN BY A TEAM OF CURRICULUM EXPERTS

WHAT IS SNAP SCIENCE?

SNAP SCIENCE IS A DYNAMIC TOOLKIT TO HELP YOU DELIVER OUTSTANDING SCIENCE THROUGHOUT YOUR SCHOOL

SIMPLE SCIENCE SOLUTIONS – making challenging concepts meaningful

HELPING EVERY CHILD ACHIEVE – with three levels of differentiated challenge

EASY TO IMPLEMENT – using the flexible planning tool enables you to plan effectively for your class

EFFECTIVE ASSESSMENT – in a world without levels

CULTIVATE A SPIRIT OF ENQUIRY – with interactive exploration and investigation activities

WRITTEN BY A TEAM OF CURRICULUM EXPERTS

MEET THE BRAINS BEHIND SNAP SCIENCE...

Series editor: Jane Turner

Jane Turner has been a primary school teacher, science outreach leader manager, LA consultant, CPD leader, and curriculum developer. Jane co-founded and is currently the Director of the Primary Science Quality Mark award scheme as well as working as Science Curriculum Advisor to the DfE Standards and Testing Agency.

Jane's team of Snap Science authors, Liz Lawrence, Naomi Hiscock, Nicola Beverley, James de Winter, and Bryony Turford are all highly experienced teachers who now work as consultants or advanced skills teachers.

HOW IS SNAP SCIENCE STRUCTURED?

YEAR GROUP/ COMPONENT	TEACHING AND ASSESSMENT TOOLKIT Delivered online via Collins Connect Platform	TEACHING FRAMEWORK Black and white, spiral bound, A4
Year 1		
Year 2		
Year 3		
Year 4		
Year 5		
Year 6		

AVAILABLE JUNE 2014

AVAILABLE JANUARY 2014

AVAILABLE APRIL 2014

PACKED WITH REAL-LIFE IMAGES AND DETAILED ILLUSTRATIONS

Digestion starts in the mouth

Spit makes the food easy to swallow and starts to break it up into even smaller pieces.

teeth

tongue

mouth

EFFECTIVE ASSESSMENT

Built-in formative assessment throughout supports teachers in tracking progress, recording judgements and providing evidence of learning.

PLANNING

Raise pupil achievement

ASSESSMENT

TEACHING

THE SNAP SCIENCE SOLUTION

✓ 2014 Curriculum matched

✓ Straightforward pricing that offers great value for money

✓ Rigorously tested and developed

✓ Progression for every child

✓ Effective assessment

✓ Supports the development of your school curriculum

EASY TO IMPLEMENT

With a simple drag-and-drop planning tool at your disposal, planning for your lesson and across the term is easy.

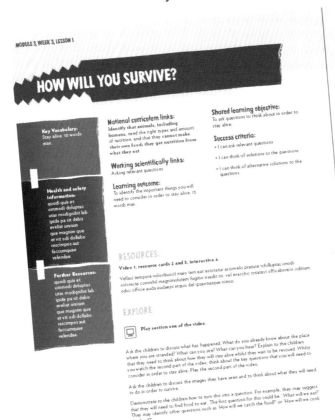

MODULE 3, WEEK 3, LESSON 1

HOW WILL YOU SURVIVE?

Key Vocabulary:
Stay alive. 10 words max.

Health and safety information:
quodi quis et ommodi doluptas utas modignihit lab ipide pa sit debis eveliat ureium que magnim que et vit odi dollabo rescimpos aut faccumque velendae.

Further Resources:
quodi quis et ommodi doluptas utas modignihit lab ipide pa sit debis eveliat ureium que magnim que et vit odi dollabo rescimpos aut faccumque velendae.

National curriculum links:
Identify that animals, including humans, need the right types and amount of nutrition, and that they cannot make their own food; they get nutrition from what they eat

Working scientifically links:
Asking relevant questions

Learning outcome:
To identify the important things you will need to consider in order to stay alive. 15 words max.

Shared learning objective:
To ask questions to think about in order to stay alive.

Success criteria:
• I can ask relevant questions
• I can think of solutions to the questions
• I can think of alternative solutions to the questions

RESOURCES:
Video 1, resource cards 2 and 3, Interactive 4.

Vellaci tempore voloribuscil maio tem eat estotatur assinvelis prature rchilluptas imodi solsrecta comnihil magnimolutem fugitio nsedit mi, vel everchic totatest officaberero oditium odici officie auda audaept atquis id ipsantiatque nimus.

EXPLORE

Play section one of the video.

Ask the children to discuss what has happened. What do you already know about the place where you are stranded? What can you see? What can you hear? Explain to the children that they need to think about how they will stay alive whilst they wait to be rescued. Whilst you watch the second part of the video, think about the key questions that you will need to consider in order to stay alive. Play the second part of the video.

Ask the children to discuss the images they have seen and to think about what they will need to do in order to survive.

Demonstrate to the children how to turn this into a question. For example, they may suggest that they will need to find food to eat. The first question for this could be 'What will we eat?' They may identify other questions such as 'How will we catch the food?' or 'How will we cook the food?'

ENQUIRE

Challenge 1
In pairs provide these children with prompt questions on cards resource_M05_CL01_asset2. Ask the children to discuss what they will need to do to address these questions. Ask them to record their ideas in drawings and by writing sentences on the back of the card. If time, ask them to think about which problems they should deal with first.

Challenge 2
In pairs provide these children with prompt questions on cards, resource_M05_CL01_asset3. Ask the children to discuss what they will need to do to address these questions. Ask them to write down any additional questions that arise as they discuss their solutions. Ask them to record their ideas by writing sentences on the back of the cards. If time, ask them to think about which problems they should deal with first.

Challenge 3
In pairs, ask these children to think of four key questions that they will need to consider in _____ the island. Provide them with a sheet of _____. Ask them to write one quest _____ discuss their solutions. Ask _____ those they later discard an _____ arise. If time, ask them to _____ should deal with first.

REFLECT AND _____
Display the six quest _____ 2 (interactive_M05 _____ questions that you _____ to stay alive? Add _____ partner which you _____ about first and wh _____ children to share _____ order as appropri _____ priority? Ensure _____ need water and _____ addressed first _____ and will be a _____

EVIDENCE OF LEARNING:
Do all the children understand that we need to eat and drink water in order to stay alive? Were the children completing challenge 2 and 3 able to write relevant questions? Were the children able to think of solutions to the questions? Were the children able to think of alternative solutions to the questions? Were the children able to explain why one solution may be better than another? Were the children able to put the tasks in order of importance?

CROSS CURRICULA OPPORTUNITIES:
Modiatut, te pliqui veliquasi tapiden ihillup tatius illoreiumqui temporionet vit, iunto es rem ratatata quid mi, sam eaquam que dolut et la pore nihilique cum reptaep erfera venditusam, occusci simi, volum et omnist, con rerum eatas evenimin cus culpari hictussimint ipsanditatur sum hilis aut atuscil ea expliquame culliqu aes cils es.

Big Cat book link:

Resources briefs:
Please use asset briefing sheets supplied.

Collins Connect — SNAP SCIENCE

My Teaching Plan

National Curriculum Programme of Study	Lesson Objectives	Lesson(s)

Teach and assess	Resources

TEEMING WITH ENQUIRY BASED, HANDS-ON ACTIVITIES, AS WELL AS VIDEOS, IMAGES AND MORE BRINGING EVERY LESSON TO LIFE!

HOW DO I FIND OUT MORE?

Contact your Snap Science consultant:
www.collinseducation.com/findyourrep

Register your interest online to be kept up-to-date with Snap Science:
www.collinseducation.com/snapscience

AND FOR THOSE SUPER KEEN SCIENTISTS OUT THERE YOU CAN PRE-REGISTER YOUR INTEREST TO EVALUATE SNAP SCIENCE WITH YOUR CLASS!

☐ I would like to evaluate Snap Science - 9780007939176

YOUR DETAILS:

Name: ....

Position: ....

School name and address: ....

Postcode: ....

Telephone: ....

Email: ....

Return to:
Collins, HarperCollins Publishers,
FREEPOST PAM6429, 77-85 Fulham Palace Road, London, W6 8JB

Email: education.marketing@harpercollins.co.uk

RL4006

3.9 Male or female authors?

More books are written by men because people prefer male writers.

The best books are written by men because men have the best imaginations.

The best books are written by women because only women are able to write about female characters.

Women have more responsibilities, so they don't have as much time to write.

What do YOU think?

Look at 50 fiction books chosen at random. How many are written by men and how many by women? What about non-fiction? Does it depend when they were written? Do men seem to write certain types of book and women others? Does the target age of the reader make a difference? Write a list of your 10 favourite books. Are there more male or female authors on the list? Do you expect books written by women to be different from those written by men? In what ways, and why? Can you tell the difference?

In the past, most women had limited opportunities to be writers. Even now, some publishers view male authors more seriously or think people may be reluctant to read stories written by women. There are women who have chosen to write using a male name (George Elliot), and others who have used initials (J. K. Rowling). There are males who choose to hide their gender too. Some people think that males find it hard to fully describe a female's feelings or experiences, and vice versa. Some people think that women write about emotion better than men. Not everybody agrees with these views. Is there any difference in the way males and females usually write about emotions, humour, crime or factual information? How do you know? Look at some samples of different types of writing; including ones written by young people. See if you can identify if a male or female wrote each piece. Do you all agree?

3.10 How do you choose a book?

Think about the last book that you read. How did you choose it? Can you remember the title or what was on the cover? Did it illustrate the story or make you wonder what was going to happen? Did you read the blurb? What do you think the purpose of the blurb is? Did you read the first page, or flick through the book, to decide if you wanted to read it? What else have you done to choose a book? Talk with your group about how you each decide which book to choose. Are your answers the same or different?

There isn't a best way of deciding which book to read. Surveys show that there are lots of different ways to choose a book, but the subject and the author tend to be very important. Some people look at reviews first, or read books that someone else has recommended. Authors and publishers spend a lot of time and effort choosing titles, designing covers and writing blurbs because they know how important these can be in persuading readers to choose their books. Sometimes people choose a book using one of these strategies and then they are disappointed with the book. Ask a selection of people that you know who are older and younger than you how they choose a book and which strategies are the most helpful. Based on your findings, what would you advise a publisher or author to do?

Books and the art of writing

Stylistic devices

4

4

Stylistic devices

4.1 Alliteration

Look for different examples of alliteration in non-fiction texts, stories, poems, posters and other writing. Where do you find them? Think about phrases that you always remember. Do any of them use alliteration? Where is it used most often? If alliterations can be hard to say, why is it ever a good idea to use them? In what situations do you think alliteration is most effective? Discuss your ideas with others in your class. Have a challenge between teams in your class to find as many alliterations as you can during one week.

Alliteration is the repetition of a particular sound in the first syllable(s) of a series of words. It is used for effect, especially in rhymes such as *Betty Botter bought some butter, but she said the butter's bitter* ... It is also found in other situations, such as advertisements and brand names, sports teams, cartoon characters and popular songs. Alliteration helps to make phrases flow so they are easy to remember. Even well known expressions use alliteration − *busy as a bee* or *good as gold* are examples. See what these examples sound like if you change the words to remove the alliteration. Which is most effective? Write some alliterations of your own for different purposes. Share them with others in your group. What do they think about your examples? What improvements can they suggest?

Stylistic devices

4.2 What is a simile?

Find out what a simile is. Make a small collection of similes. Are they all the same? Do they use the same kinds of words? Why do you think that some similes say something is *like* something else, but others say it is *as* ...... *as* something else? Do you think one way of writing similes is better than the other? Are all the similes you found funny? Do you all agree? Try to work out some rules for writing similes. Do they work for all the similes you found?

Similes are comparisons. They show how two things that are not alike in most ways are similar in one important way. Similes generally use the words *as* or *like* to make the connection between the two things that are being compared. Some similes are funny because they make ridiculous suggestions (like a chocolate teapot), but they don't have to be funny. How many different similes can you find or write about one thing – the Sun, a river, an eye, an animal? How many different ways can you complete a simile such as *as quick as, as soft as, as miserable as*? Try them out on your friends. Are they all similes? What improvements can they suggest?

4.3 Using similes

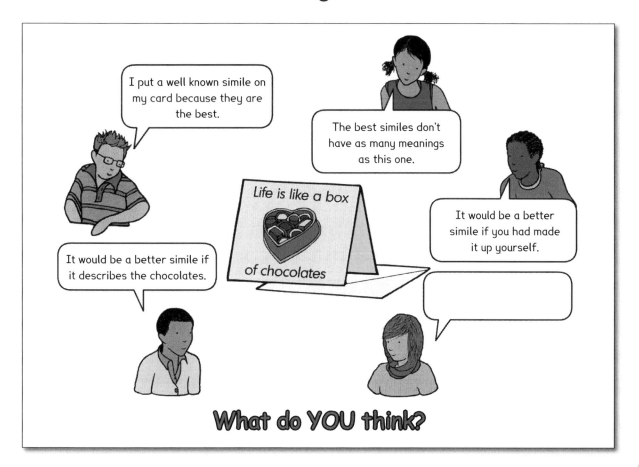

How many meanings can you think of for *Life is like a box of chocolates*? Find other examples of similes. What do you think they mean? Do they all have more than one meaning? If a simile can be interpreted in many ways, does that make it a good or a bad simile? If the reader has seen or heard a simile many times, does this make it more effective? Find similes in pieces of writing and change them for new ones that you have made up. What effect does that have on the meaning?

Some similes don't have much impact because they are really obvious or well known – for example, *as slow as a snail*. They can be more effective if they are exaggerated by adding extra detail, like *as slow as a snail with its brakes on.* Make a list of well known similes and improve them by adding more detail. An original simile can be even more effective, especially if you can make an unusual comparison. For example, instead of *as thin as a stick*, think of other things that are thin: *as thin as a dieting ant's antenna* or *as thin as a hair on a hungry hare's back*. Have a competition with your group to create unique similes. Which are the most effective? Sometimes using similes with several meanings can make writing more interesting. Which of yours can be used to give the writing more than one meaning? When is this useful?

4.4 What is a metaphor?

Research the meanings of simile and metaphor. What is the difference between them? Find some examples of both and discuss which is which with your group to make sure you all understand the difference. How can you decide if a figure of speech is a metaphor? Take some similes and try to turn them into metaphors. What do you have to do? Does a metaphor always have to include two nouns? Can you find any that don't?

A metaphor says one thing is another thing, such as *her hair was rats' tails*. This is more powerful than a simile, which says one thing is like another. A metaphor usually creates a much stronger image in the reader's head than a simile. For example, if you said *her feet were blocks of ice*, this creates a mental picture of a girl with blocks of ice instead of feet and this is much more memorable than just saying her feet are cold. Lots of metaphors create connections between nouns, but you can use verbs in metaphors too, such as *I wolfed my lunch today*. Create some metaphors and use these to draw some amusing pictures. Share them with others in your group. What improvements can they suggest?

Stylistic devices

4.5 Using metaphors

Find examples of metaphors in some stories. What kind of images do they create? How useful are they in the writing? Do any of the metaphors make the descriptions funny? Is this the only use they have? Does the writing get better if there are more metaphors? Would you prefer it if some of them weren't there? Choose some of the metaphors you have found. Try replacing them with a more standard description. How does that change the feel of the story?

We use metaphors to create strong images in writing. These might be funny, or they might create other emotions for the reader, and both of these will make your writing more interesting. Metaphors can make you think too, by making unexpected connections between things. If you look back at some stories you have written, you can probably see places where you could have included a metaphor to make your writing more interesting. Create some metaphors and add them to your writing. Try using different styles. They could be funny metaphors, frightening, sad, surprising, and so on. What do your friends think about them? Have they improved your writing?

4.6 Personification

Find out what personification means and look at some examples. Highlight the word or phrase that is the personification. Can you find ways to group the examples according to the actions and qualities used? Is one quality used more frequently? Are there more opportunities to use happy human qualities for personification? What about more negative feelings like anger? Are there any human qualities that did not occur? Are you surprised about this? Think about what you have noticed about personification and discuss the possible reasons. How is personification different from, and similar to, a metaphor?

Personification is a figure of speech in which the writer gives human qualities, feelings, actions or characteristics to something that isn't human. For example, *The old tree is an aged and tired man; its knobbly fingers tremble, reaching out.* In this example, the writer uses a series of metaphors and gives the tree human qualities, so this is an example of personification. Discuss how effective you think this is. Make a list of objects and another list of verbs that are human actions – laughing, giggling, and so on. Now put the two together as if you are bringing the objects alive e.g. *the clock glared down.* How can using personification make something seem frightening? What other effects can it have? Discuss with your group how your examples could be used in writing and try them out.

4.7 Onomatopoeia

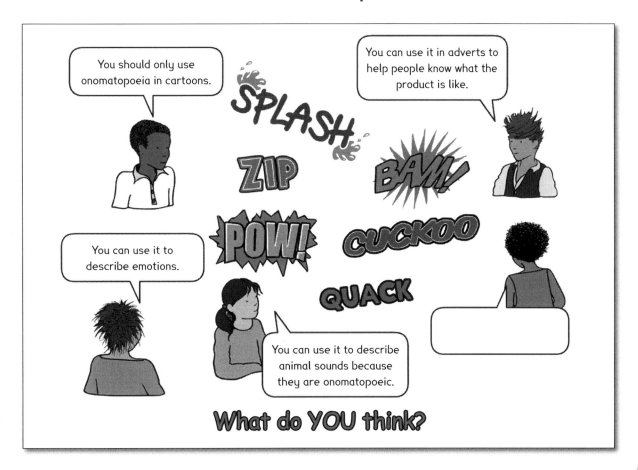

Find out what the word onomatopoeia means, think about where you have seen it used and find some examples. In what sorts of stories do you find onomatopoeic words? Are they ever found in poetry? What about non-fiction texts? Where are onomatopoeic words most frequently found? Why are they used in these situations? What effect is the writer hoping for? Look at as many examples as you can, and discuss how they have been used and how effective you think they are.

Onomatopoeia is where a word is used that sounds like the thing it is describing. Examples of onomatopoeia are *buzz* to describe the sound that a bee makes, *pop* to describe the sound that a paper bag makes when it bursts, and *gurgle* to describe the sound of water going down a plug hole. If you make a list of onomatopoeic words then you should be able to divide them into categories (e.g. animal noises, collisions, liquid sounds, etc.) and look for patterns in the type of letter sounds used. Writers sometimes create their own onomatopoeic words. Try creating some examples of onomatopoeia and use them in sentences. How well do other people think that they work? Do onomatopoeic words exist in different languages?

55

4.8 Humour

Think about what makes you laugh when you are reading a book. Is it the way something is described? Are particular words funny? Make a list of words that you find funny and compare it with lists made by others in your group. Can you see any similarities in the sorts of words you have chosen? Can a word on its own be funny or does it have to be in a sentence or phrase? What makes a situation funny? Is it the situation itself, the way it is described or what it is compared to? Find some examples and see if you can work out how the humour is created.

Different people laugh at different things. What you find funny may be very different from what your friend finds funny, which makes it quite challenging to create humour. It is more difficult to be funny in writing than in oral situations. In conversation, facial expressions, tone of voice, body language, and sounds can all be used to create humour. Creating humour in writing relies solely on the way words are used. This is not easy to achieve. Try writing some humorous similes by choosing a word that contrasts with the adjective (e.g. *as cuddly as a cactus, or as speedy as a snail*). Experiment with other strategies to create humorous pieces of writing. Which do you think work best for you? Share them with others in your group. What improvements can they suggest?

Spelling

5

5

Spelling

5.1 Plural?

Do you understand what it says on the sign? If you do, why do you think they are arguing about the spellings? Look up some nouns and their plurals. What kind of endings do they have to make them plural? Group the words and see if you can find patterns in the way that you make them plural. Are there any words that do not fit the patterns? Do you all agree?

There are several ways of forming plurals. Different words have different rules. For many nouns you just add s, but it is not as simple as that. If words end in x, s, z, ch, sh, then usually you add es. Words ending in o can have either e or es added to make them plural. Words ending in a vowel and y usually have s added. Words ending in a consonant and y usually lose the y and have ies added. If the word ends in f or fe then these are removed and ves is normally added. Not all words fit these rules. For example, some words do not have anything added but the word is changed in a different way. Words that fit the rules are known as regular plurals and the rest are called irregular plurals. Collect sets of words that fit each rule and those that don't. What strategies can you think of to help you remember which rule to use?

5.2 Leafs

Do you understand what the sign says? If you understand what the sign says, do you think that the spelling matters? Look up some nouns and their plurals. Look at the kinds of endings they have to make them plural. Group the words and see if you can find patterns in the way that you make them plural. Do words ending in f have different plurals from the other words? Are there any words that do not fit the pattern? Do you all agree?

There are different ways of forming plurals. Different words have different rules. If a word ends in f then usually the f is removed and ves added. For example, shelf becomes shelves. If a word ends in fe then usually the fe is removed and ves added. For example, life becomes lives. If a word ends in ff then usually s is added. For example, cliff becomes cliffs. The correct spelling on the sign should be leaves. There are some exceptions to this rule, such as roof, proof and chief, that become roofs, proofs and chiefs. What strategies can you think of to help you remember which rule to use?

5.3 Adverbs

Which word would you use in your writing? Talk about what kind of word 'accidently' is and what word it comes from. If it is an adverb does that help you to understand how it might be spelt? See if you can think of other words that have a similar ending. Does this help you to decide on which spelling is most likely? The spelling of some words is shorter and simpler in US English than UK English. Do you think there might be different spellings of 'accidently' in UK English and US English? Try looking up each spelling of the word in a UK English and a US English dictionary.

Accidentally is the correct spelling of the word. It's the adverb from accidental, so accidental becomes accidentally. It's just like typical, where the adverb is typically, not typicly, or incidental and incidentally. When we pronounce accidentally we often say it with four syllables, rather than five, so it often sounds more like 'accidently' than 'accidentally'. This can cause confusion with the spelling. Some dictionaries now accept accidently as correct, which makes it even more confusing! What other words can you find that follow this rule?

5.4 Silent letters

Discuss what you know about silent letters. Think of examples of silent letters at the beginning, middle and ends of words. Look up some more examples on the internet. Group the words and see if you can find any patterns in what the silent letters do. Is there any difference in what silent letters do when they come at the end of a word? Does where the silent letter comes in the word make any difference to what the silent letter does? Are there any words that don't fit this pattern? Do you all agree?

The English language has a lot of silent letters, and this makes spelling more complicated and confusing than it is in many other languages. Sometimes silent letters change the pronunciation of a word. Examples of these are rat and rate, were and where. Sometimes silent letters change the meaning of a word. Examples of these are night and knight, to and two. Sometimes groups of letters go together to make a single sound, where the sound is different from each of the individual letters. Examples of these are gh (e.g. rough, laugh) and ph (e.g. physical, phantom). There are lots of silent letters that don't really do much at all. Examples of these are double consonants (e.g. stuff, horrid, hello) and letters that are not sounded (e.g. b in doubt or lamb, w in answer, c in scenic). Make a chart of common words with silent letters to help you remember them.

5.5 Council or counsel

Can you think of any occasions when you have used the word 'council' or 'counsel'? Discuss whether you think this is two words with different meanings, or just one word with different spellings. With some words the noun and the verb are spelt differently. Do you think that applies here? Look up both spellings in a dictionary and see what it says. Are you surprised? What about 'counsellors' and 'councillors'? Can you work out what those words must mean? Make a list of words where the noun and the verb are spelt differently.

The notice on the newsstand is correct. The sentence is a lovely example of the correct use of council/counsel and councillor/counsellor. A council is a body or group that makes decisions, such as Liverpool City Council, and a councillor is a person who is a member of that council. Counsel is advice, often legal advice. To counsel is to give advice. A counsellor is a person who gives advice. So what the notice on the newsstand means is that the councillors need counselling. Try creating a short piece of writing where you use correctly the words council and counsel.

63

5.6 i before e

See if you can find out more about this rule, and when and why it was created. Do you ever use this rule when trying to decide on a spelling? Find as many words as you can where there is an ie or ei, including those that follow a c. How often does the spelling break the rule? If a rule doesn't apply all the time, why do you think it exists? When does a rule like this stop being useful? Are there ways of making it more useful?

The full rhyme is *'i before e, except after c, or when sounded as "a", as in neighbour and weigh'*. The i before e rule only applies to words that have an 'ee' sound, such as thief, priest or achieve. When the 'ee' sound comes after c, as in receive, ceiling and deceit, or the words have an 'ay' sound, as in eight or vein, then the spelling is ei. However, there are some exceptions to the rule, such as protein and seize. Can you work out a way of remembering which words are exceptions? Discuss other spelling rules that you know. Which ones are useful to you? Try to make up a rule that would help you spell certain words more accurately, then try these rules in your group to see which work best.

5.7 Remembering spellings

Think about the last time you had a spelling test. How difficult was it to memorise the words? Did you try using different ways of learning the spellings? How many different ways are there to learn spellings? How many do you need to know to be a good speller? Is a spell checker always right? Choose some words and discuss with your group how each of you would learn how to spell them. How many different methods do you use?

There are lots of different ways to learn spellings. Everyone learns differently, so it is important that you work out which ways help you the most. Some people learn by using phonics. You can try breaking words down into chunks of sounds. You can learn rules for the tricky part of a word. Sometimes the rhythm of a word helps you to remember the spelling. The shape of a word can help, and linking to other words with similar spellings can help too. Some people find it helpful to learn the word as part of a sentence. Some methods will be better for certain words, but not necessarily for all words. Do you have any other ways of learning spellings? The more ways you can use, the better your spelling will be. Talk about which methods sound most useful, try them out and see which appear to be most successful.

5.8 Incorrect spelling

Why do you think this shop chose to use the spelling fone instead of phone? Look for examples of other words that are spelt differently from how they are in the dictionary. Do you think writers mean to use different spellings for some words, or do they just make a mistake? Create a list of common words and alternative spellings that are used for them. Do they all make sense?

It is important to know the correct way of spelling a word, but writers sometimes deliberately choose to use a different spelling. Writers do this to create an effect, such as making the reader notice the word more. There are increasing numbers of words used in everyday life that are deliberately misspelt. Examples include the names of companies, toys, games, breakfast cereals and song titles. Language changes over time, so words like *fone* may eventually appear in the dictionaries. Some people argue that it doesn't really matter if the word is incorrectly spelt, as long as the reader can understand it. Do you agree? Can you think of any situations when you might spell a word incorrectly, or should you always use the word as it is spelt in the dictionary? What might happen if children grow up only learning alternative spellings of words, such as *nite* for *night* and *lite* for *light*? What do you think about using American spellings such as color and favorite? Create guidelines for when alternative spellings are acceptable.

5.9 Spelling made-up words

Will you know that the planet is called Zito if it is spelt Pzxg? If not, how do you feel about this? If you don't know how to say a word, does that change your enjoyment of the story? Look in some books for made-up words. Did you find any with confusing spellings? When you read a word you have never seen before, how do you decide how to pronounce it? If you are reading silently, do you try to say the word in your head, or do you just ignore how it sounds? What impact on the reader do you think writers try to create with made-up words? When a writer makes up a word, should they think about how the reader will pronounce it?

Writers sometimes use made-up words for nouns, adjective and verbs. Normally they use spellings that help the reader to pronounce the words, even if the reader has not seen the words before. Sometimes a word might be created in order to confuse the reader or to make them stop and think. Some readers might find this irritating and feel that it spoils the flow of the story. When you make up a word you should have a clear reason for doing so and think carefully about the reader. The way you choose to spell it should be influenced by its purpose. Create some sentences containing made-up words of your own, and discuss their impact and meaning with your group.

5.10 Spelling phonetically

Can you read and understand what is written above the trough in the picture? Why is this, when none of the words are spelt correctly? How do you think they should be spelt? If people can write words so everyone can understand them, what is the point of having dictionaries? Are there times when you should try to write a word even if you are not sure how to spell it? Look at some sentences that were written using the wrong letter combinations for the sounds in those words. Your teacher will give you some. What do you think the correct spellings are? How do you know?

Sometimes you want to use a word in your writing and you are not sure how to spell it. If a dictionary isn't available, you can use your knowledge of other words to get as close as possible to the correct spelling so that the reader knows which word it is. You can use sounds that you know to help you construct the word. The writer of the text above the trough has tried to do this, but has used the wrong letters (graphemes) for the sounds (phonemes) in those words. There may be some smaller sections within the word that you can spell. Take it in turns to say some challenging words to each other to spell. After writing them, discuss how you decided what to write. Look at the correct spelling and talk about how to remember the spelling in future.

5.11 Texting

Think about how you spell the words you use when you text. How do you decide on the spelling? Does texting have its own spelling rules? Are they written down anywhere? If they exist but not everyone knows them, does this matter? If texting is not writing, then what is it? Look at some texts and discuss with others whether they are written in formal or informal language. Is your decision about whether language is formal or informal based on spelling? Do you think it is important to spell correctly, whatever the situation?

There are no set rules for texting. The language and spellings that you use may vary depending on who you are texting. Sometimes the way that you text will be similar to how you write, but often texting and writing follow different rules and spelling conventions. The spellings you use may also depend on the availability of software such as predictive text. Spellings in standard written English have evolved over time. Spelling conventions in texting also change. Do you think that texting is having any impact on written English? People have negative and positive views about the impact of texting on young people's ability to spell English words correctly. What evidence can you find to support either view? Carry out a survey to find out what younger and older people think about this.

5.12 Confusing spellings

Do you think that there is any problem with how the word *there* is spelt in the headline? What do you think the problem is, and why do you think it might have happened? Use a dictionary to help you check the spellings. Does the word *there* have more than one meaning? Can words have more than one meaning? Can you think of any everyday words that have several different meanings? Look in a dictionary if it helps. Share your words with others. Some words sound the same but are spelt differently. How many of these can you find?

There are many words that sound the same but have different meanings and are spelt differently, such as they're, there and their in the headline. They are called homophones. Other examples of these words are to, too and two; so and sew; pour, poor and pore. It can be difficult to decide which spelling to use. Other words are spelt the same but have more than one meaning, such as trip, which can mean a journey or to fall over something. These are called homographs. Usually it is obvious which meaning to apply when you are reading, but sometimes it is confusing. It helps if you can think of a way to remember the meanings and when to use each one. Look at the homophones and homographs that you found. Work together to think of ways of remembering how to spell these words and what they mean.

Punctuation

Punctuation

6.1 Why punctuate?

Find some examples of sentences with a lot of punctuation. Write them out without the punctuation and get someone else to read them aloud. Do you think they will read the sentences differently if the punctuation is there? Does it change the meaning at all? Look at the sentences again. Add some different punctuation. What difference does it make? What about the same punctuation, but in different places? Which type of punctuation do you think makes the biggest difference to the meaning of a piece of writing?

When we speak we use strategies such as pauses, tone of voice and facial expressions to help listeners understand what we mean and make it interesting for them. We can't use these strategies when we write, but we can use punctuation. Punctuation helps writing to flow and makes it easier to read. It also makes writing more interesting and helps the reader to understand what the writer means. Changing the punctuation can change the meaning of a sentence. For example: *Can we eat Nana? Can we eat, Nana?* or *You will be late. You will be late?* As a writer you need to be sure that your meaning is clear to the reader. Look at some of your recent writing and edit it to improve your use of punctuation, to make your writing more interesting and make your meaning clearer. What do your friends think about the changes you made?

6.2 Deciding on punctuation

Think about other ways of punctuating the words *Silence test in progress*. Write the words out in different ways, each time putting in different punctuation or putting the punctuation in a different place. Talk with your group about how to change the meaning by changing the punctuation. Do you agree on the best choice of punctuation, or do you have different ideas? Are you clear about the purpose of each punctuation mark? Is it sometimes better to change the word order, rather than adding extra punctuation? Try it and see what happens.

The best way to show the meaning of the statement is to write it as: *Silence, test in progress.* There are other ways to write it – for example, *Silence! Test in progress.* When you write, sometimes there is only one punctuation mark that should be used. There are other situations when you have to make decisions about whether punctuation is needed and what kind to use. In these situations, remember that the purpose of punctuation is to make your meaning absolutely clear to the reader. In the example below, would you choose to use brackets, commas or dashes?
· *The robber (Sneeky Snatchem) escaped from the police.*
· *The robber, Sneeky Snatchem, escaped from the police.*
· *The robber – Sneeky Snatchem – escaped from the police.*
How can you decide which is the best punctuation to use and when?

6.3 Commas

Think about what you already know about commas. Look at a piece of writing and find as many different places as you can where there are commas. Try to sort them according to the different ways they are used. How many different ways can you find? Do you think they have been used correctly? Share any that you think are wrong, and see if you all agree.

A comma has more than one use. It can be used to separate words in lists, around a drop-in clause (where the words enclosed by the commas could be left out without changing the general meaning of the sentence) and before the causal connectives *or, but, yet, while*. Sometimes it is used before the word *and*, but not always. Commas are also used when writing numbers, dates and addresses. They should make it easier to read the sentence and help the writer to make their meaning clear to the reader. Find some examples of all of these uses. Practise writing some of your own. Can you use a comma in all of these ways in one piece of writing? Try it. How difficult was it to do, and why? Create your own dictionary definition for a comma. Share with others and see if they agree with your definition.

6.4 Using commas for meaning

Do you think Mollie and Max are dogs or people? Could they be dogs? Could they be people? Can you re-write the sentence so it is clear that Mollie and Max are dogs? Can you re-write it again so it is clear that they are people? Can you re-write it so that one is a dog and one is a person? Would it be better to write the sentence in a different way? How would you write it? Try reading sentences with and without commas. What difference do the commas make?

Changing the placement of a comma can change the meaning of a sentence. Using them accurately helps to make your intended meaning clear. You can also make your meaning clear by rewriting the sentence. For example: *I went to the park with my dogs named Mollie and Max. I went to the park with my dogs and my friends Mollie and Max.*

Discuss how the meaning of this sentence has been changed by moving the commas.
- *The old lady collected all sorts of things: silver, paper, hats and clocks.*
- *The old lady collected all sorts of things: silver paper, hats, and clocks.*
- *The old lady collected all sorts of things: silver, paper hats, and clocks.*

How many examples of writing can you find where a comma can change the meaning? Create some examples of how a comma can change the meaning of a phrase or sentence, and try them out on your friends.

6.5 Comma or semi-colon?

Look in some books to see where commas and semi-colons are used. List the ways that they are used. Think about what you already know about using semi-colons and commas. How do you decide whether a semi-colon is better than two separate sentences? Can you ever use a comma instead of a semi-colon, or do they have different uses? Are there any words that you could use instead of a semi-colon? Would you need a comma if you use the *but* before *we*? Try joining some sentences together by using semi-colons. Do they still make sense?

A semi-colon should be used to join two complete sentences into a single sentence. However, it is often used incorrectly, such as *I don't like him; not at all.* Talk about why this is wrong. Commas can also be used incorrectly to join two sentences together, as in the note Class 5 wrote to the caretaker. Commas are normally used where two sentences are joined together using words such as *or, but, yet* or *while*. Look through some of your own work, as well as some other texts, to find examples of semi-colons and commas. Talk about whether semi-colons have been used correctly to join sentences together. Would you change the way that any of them are used? Would you use words instead? Try to work out how to remember the most effective ways of using commas and semi-colons.

Punctuation

6.6 Colons and semi-colons

Look through some books and find where authors have used a colon or a semi-colon. List the different ways that they have been used. Do all authors use them in the same way? Check the rules for using colons and semi-colons. Do any authors break these rules? Why do you think they might do this? Talk about how you can decide whether to use a semi-colon or a colon. Try using colons and semi-colons in some writing. Share what you have done with your friends. Do they agree with how you have used them?

A colon is often used to introduce a list of items, as shown here. *Things to bring for the trip: a packed lunch, something to drink and a pair of wellies.* The first part of the sentence tells you that there will be things to bring; then the colon tells you 'here are the things'. You can also use a colon to introduce an explanation or a definition of something. *Elephant: a large grey mammal found in Africa and India.* A semi-colon is often used to join together two sentences. *Jamil won a pen; Trish won a bike.* These could be separate sentences, but a semi-colon suggests that there is a relationship between the sentences. Look at some of your recent writing, and other texts, to see if you can find places where you can use colons or semi-colons. Check with others to see if they agree.

6.7 When to use an apostrophe

Discuss in your group why you think apostrophes are used. What difference does it make if they are missing? Look at how apostrophes are used in a book and see if you can work out why the writer has used apostrophes. Now look in another book and see if the same rules are being used. Is the market trader using the same rules on the sign? Create some signs that need apostrophes and some that do not. Swap your signs with other friends. Do you agree about how you have used the apostrophes?

Apostrophes should never be used before the s in plurals. This means that the sign saying *carrot's and onion's* is wrong. Apostrophes are used to show where there are letters missing (for example, I **cannot** come to the party becomes I **can't** come to the party). Apostrophes are also used to show possession. In the sentence *Jenny's ice cream is melting*, the ice cream belongs to Jenny and there is only one Jenny, so the apostrophe goes before the 's'. When there is more than one person the apostrophe goes after the 's', as in *The boys' cloakroom is very untidy*. The cloakroom belongs to more than one boy. Check your writing to see if you use apostrophes correctly. Look for plurals and make sure you have not used apostrophes by mistake. Create your own set of rules to help you remember where to use apostrophes.

6.8 Its or it's?

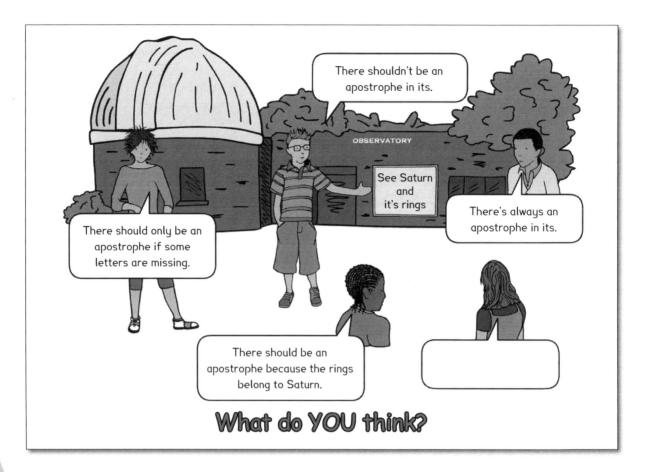

Talk about why apostrophes might be used in the word *it's*. What difference would it make if the apostrophe was missing? Look in a book for the words *it's* and *its*. What rule does the writer seem to be using to decide whether or not to use an apostrophe? Have a look in another book and see if the same rule is being used. Write some sentences using *it's* and *its*. Share your writing with a friend and talk about why you used each word. Do you agree with each other?

Usually we use apostrophes to show that there are letters missing or to show possession. *Its* is an exception to this rule. There is only an apostrophe when its means it is or it has. For example *It's very sunny today* means *It is very sunny today*. We don't use an apostrophe with *its* to show possession. For example, *The cat has eaten all its food* means that the cat has eaten all the food that belongs to it. This means that the sign outside the observatory is wrong. It should be *See Saturn and its rings*. A good test is to see if you can replace *it's* with *it is* or *it has*. If you can, then it needs an apostrophe. Set your friends a challenge by writing some sentences using *it's* and *its* where some are wrong. Talk about how to remember which version to use, and create your own rules for using apostrophes.

6.9 Exclamation marks

Think about what you already know about exclamation marks and why they are used in writing. Find as many different places as you can where exclamation marks are used. Try to sort them into the different ways that they are used. Are exclamation marks only used to show emotions? What about at the end of a command? Are there more exclamation marks in certain genres than in others? Are exclamation marks used more frequently in speech than in prose? Find some examples to support your answers. Do you think exclamation marks improve writing? If so, why?

A sentence that gives a command or shows strong emotions, like surprise, anger or joy, ends with an exclamation mark. For example, *After months of careful work, the archaeologists finally opened the tomb. It was empty!* It can show strong feelings or a raised voice. It is often used in short phrases or with single words, like *Go away!* or *Stop!* The exclamation mark can make what is written mean different things. Sometimes in informal writing more than one exclamation mark is used: *It was so amazing!!!!* Can you think of situations when this might be acceptable? You should avoid using exclamation marks in formal writing, unless absolutely necessary. Why do you think this is? Can you ever use another punctuation mark with an exclamation mark? Make up some rules for making the best use of exclamation marks.

81

6.10 Question marks

Talk about when you might need to use a question mark. Look at different pieces of writing to find examples of question marks. Try to sort them into the different ways that they are used. Is there a pattern between where question marks are used and different types of questions? Do there seem to be any rules to help you to decide whether to use question marks or not? Try writing the sentence about the new buses in different ways, with and without question marks. Share what you have done in your group. Do they agree with what you have done?

There are different kinds of questions. Some need question marks. For example: Queries – *Have you got the hottest game yet?* Statements turned into questions – *You've got the hottest game in town, haven't you?* Questions inserted into sentences – *'Have you got the hottest game in town?' we wonder.* Question marks are not normally used in indirect questions. For example: *We wonder if you have got the hottest game in town.* Changing the order of the words in a sentence can make a difference to whether or not a question mark is needed. Write a list of the questions that your teacher asks during this lesson. How could you write them as direct or indirect questions? Make up some rules for remembering when and where to use question marks.

Punctuation

6.11 Hyphens

Think about hyphens and how they are used. What job does the hyphen do if you put it between little and used? Does the phrase *little used bike* mean the same as *little-used bike*? Does a *first class trip* mean the same as a *first-class trip*? Have a look at some writing to find examples of where hyphens have been used. Talk about whether the meaning would be different without the hyphens.

Hyphens are used to link words and parts of words. When you make a compound noun you put two nouns together (e.g. *aircraft*, *silkworm*, *wheelchair*). You can also make compound adjectives, but now you need to put a hyphen between the two words (e.g. *sweet-smelling*, *blue-eyed*). Hyphens are used when describing ages and lengths of time. *The 250-year-old trees* means trees that are 250 years old, but *250 year-old trees* means 250 trees that are all one year old. They are used to show when words have a combined meaning (e.g. *mother-in-law*, *T-shirt*) and when two nouns are used to create a verb (e.g. *to ice-skate*, *to booby-trap*). Think of some compound words and decide which ones need hyphens. Make up some phrases where the use of a hyphen changes the meaning, and see who can make the most amusing phrase.

6.12 Ellipsis

Think about what you know about ellipses and how they are used. What effect do you think they create? Are they only used to create effect, or can they be used in other situations? Can they replace other punctuation? What happens if you use ellipses too much? Is it lazy to use an ellipsis? Look for examples of ellipses. How do you feel at that point in the story? Does an ellipsis improve the story? Does it make you want to read on or does it annoy you? Do your friends agree?

An ellipsis shows a pause in the flow of a sentence: *John thought and thought ... and then thought some more.* It can also show where speech is interrupted: *Sally said, "Once upon a time, there was a ...". "Not another fairy tale!" groaned Pierre.* Using ellipses like this shows that Pierre did not let Sally finish her sentence. An ellipsis can also be used for dramatic effect: *It got louder and louder ... and then suddenly, there was silence.* You need to be careful not to use an ellipsis too often. Once in a story is enough, so practise using it to get the best effect. Create a guide for how to use ellipses in writing to create the best effects.

Grammar

7.1 Sentences

Look at different sentences in a book. Are they all the same length? Do they all have verbs, nouns and adjectives? What is the shortest sentence that you can find? Did you find any that are just one word? Does everybody agree that it is a sentence? Have a look at other types of books. Does the type of writing make a difference to the sentences? Write your own examples of sentences and share them with others in your class. Talk about why they are sentences.

A sentence is a group of words that makes sense on its own. In English, sentences normally contain a noun and a verb. A sentence must begin with a capital letter and end with a full-stop, question mark or exclamation mark. Sentences can be very short or very long. The length of the sentence depends on what you want to say and the effect you are trying to create. Adjectives, connectives and adverbs make sentences longer and can make them more interesting. Sentences can be simple, compound or complex. Did you spot any of these? Some writers use one word as a sentence, *Run!* for example. Not everyone agrees that this is a sentence. What do you think? Does making a sentence longer make it better? What is the shortest sentence that you can write? Does everyone agree that it is a sentence?

7.2 Paragraphs

Look for different length paragraphs in a story book. What are the longest and shortest paragraphs you can find? Why do you think some are longer than others? Look in non-fiction books. Do they have long and short paragraphs? Are some paragraphs easier to read than others? Why do you think this is? Talk about whether the paragraphs make different types of text easier to understand.

A paragraph is a collection of sentences about the same thing. Organising your sentences into paragraphs makes your writing easier to read. A paragraph can be just one sentence, more than a page or anything in between. You should start a new line after each paragraph. You may want to miss a line before you start the next paragraph. Some people like to start the first line of a new paragraph a little way in from the edge of the page. This is called an indent. When you are writing a story how do you decide when to start a new paragraph? Does it make a difference if you are writing a story or a non-narrative text? Find a long paragraph. What could you do to make it shorter? Share it with other people in your class.

7.3 Connectives

Talk about what you know about connectives and how they are used. If you are not sure use a book or the internet to help you. Investigate connectives in different pieces of writing. Look closely at the way the sentences are constructed. Try to sort them into types of connectives and where they are used. Investigate the rhythm of sentences that start with a connective and those that have connectives elsewhere. Are sentences that contain a connective always longer than those that don't? What is the shortest sentence with a connective that you can find?

Connectives are words and phrases that help to link ideas together. They can improve the flow and structure of your writing, as well as making it more interesting. Connectives are used in many ways: to explain, to compare, to add, to discuss. They can help to explain the passing of time (*before, meanwhile, whenever*) or improve explanations (*just as, due to*). One type of connective, *and*, known as a co-ordinating conjunction, can be used to create compound sentences by joining together two simple sentences. There are seven causal connectives that also do this: *for, and, nor, but, or, yet, and so*. Other connectives help you to make complex sentences. Create a display with the connectives grouped according to the situations in which they are most useful. Use them to help you improve your writing.

7.4 Starting a sentence

Look through some books to see if you can find sentences that start with *and* or *but*. Why do you think writers might use these words? Do all writers use *and* or *but* at the start of sentences? In what other ways do writers begin sentences? Try to sort some sentences into different types of starters. Why is it useful to have different ways of starting sentences?

And and *but* are types of connectives known as co-ordinating conjunctions. This means that they are used to connect two ideas together. Some people believe that you should never start a sentence with conjunctions such as *and* or *but*. However, many writers strongly disagree and think that, if *and* or *but* are used carefully, they can create interest in writing. There are many different ways to begin a sentence. These include:

·   the subject (e.g. *The time machine* ...)
·   a participle (e.g. an -ing or -ed word, like *Running for his life* ... or *Frightened by the dark* ...)
·   other connectives (e.g. *While crowds gathered* ...)
·   an adverb (e.g. *Happily skipping down the lane* ...)
·   a phrase describing when or where (e.g. *Early in the morning* ...)

Did you find examples of all of these? What other starters did you find? Write some sentences using different types of starters. Create some guidelines to help you decide which kind of starter to use and when.

7.5 Prefixes

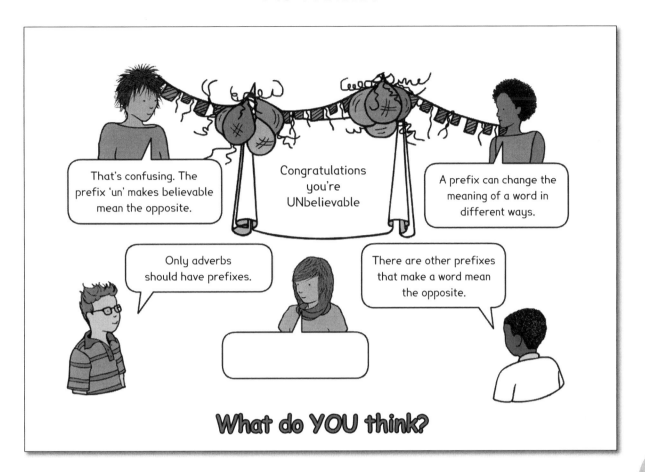

Talk about what you already know about using prefixes. If you are not sure look in a book or on the internet for how to use them. Investigate where prefixes are used. Does adding a prefix to a word always make it mean the opposite? Could it make the word mean something else? Make a list of all the words that you have found that have a prefix. What sort of words are they? Can you find any words that have more than one prefix?

A prefix is a group of letters placed at the start of a root word to modify or change its meaning. Some commonly found prefixes are: anti-, in-, im-, sub-, un-, il-, ir. All of these can change the meaning of a word so it means the opposite. Adding a prefix does not always make a word mean the opposite; they can also have different effects on the root word. Prefixes can be added to nouns, verbs and adjectives. Some words have more than one prefix. Did you find any? Although prefixes can be added to lots of words, they can't be added to every word. Create some new words by adding prefixes to words that you know. Can others in your group work out what your new word might mean? Make a class prefix word bank, with their meanings, to help you with your writing.

7.6 Suffixes

Look at different kinds of writing to investigate where suffixes are used. If you are not certain about suffixes use a book or the internet to help you. Why are they added to words? Can there be too many or too few of them? Compare words before and after suffixes have been added to them. Are the words used differently in a sentence after the suffix is added? In what ways does adding a suffix change the meaning of a word? Can you find any words that have both a suffix and a prefix?

A suffix is an ending that is added to a root word to form a new word. Commonly found suffixes are: -ful, -less, -ly, -ment, -ness, -ish, -ation, -ing. Although suffixes can be added to lots of words, they can't be added to every word. Some words have both a prefix and a suffix (e.g. *untruthful*), or more than one suffix (e.g. *cheerfulness*). Sometimes the root word changes when the suffix is added. Can you work out any rules for these changes? You can find these rules on the internet. There are many other suffixes. How many can you find? Create some new words by adding suffixes to words that you know. Can others in your group work out what your new word might mean? Make a class suffix word bank to help you with your writing.

7.7 Adverbs

Find some examples of adverbs in different types of books. Talk about where they are in the sentences and how they were formed. How many can you find that end with -ly? Does adding -ly always create an adverb? Is that the only way of making an adverb? Where in the sentence can an adverb be placed? Can the same word be used as an adverb and an adjective? Try some out and see what happens.

Adverbs are frequently used to give more information about a verb. They tell you about how, why, when, where, etc. (e.g. *They travelled **slowly***). They can come at the beginning, at the end or part-way through a sentence. Although they are often formed by adding -ly, this is not always the case. Some words end in -ly but are not adverbs (e.g. *smelly*). Group the adverbs you found according to what they tell you about the verb (*how, why, when, where*, etc.) and whether or not they are made by adding -ly. Use this to help you with your writing. Adverbs can also be added to adjectives (*The crocodile was **very** fierce*), prepositions (*It's **just** above the horizon*) or another adverb (*We meet **quite** often*). Find some more examples of these and practise using them.

7.8 Adjectives

Talk about the purpose of adjectives. If you are not sure about adjectives use a book or the internet to help you. Look at different kinds of writing to investigate where adjectives are used. Can there ever be too many adjectives in a sentence? Find some examples of adjectives that you think are particularly effective. Why are they so successful? Discuss this with your group and create a list of very effective adjectives. Do other groups have the same words on their list? Why might thinking about all of your senses help you choose a good adjective?

Adjectives are describing words. They give you more information about the noun in the sentence. They often come before the noun (e.g. the shiny spoon) but can come after the verb (e.g. the detective seems clever). Comparative adjectives are used to compare things (e.g. the apple was harder than the pear). Superlative adjectives are used to emphasise one of a group (e.g. the biggest, the most expensive). Can you see how superlative adjectives are formed? Adjectives give more detail and interest to your writing, but need choosing carefully. The ice cream seller could certainly make the sign more interesting using some adjectives, such as tasty, delicious or yummy. Try adding different adjectives to a sentence you have written. Discuss your choices with your group. Which ones do they think are most effective, and why?

Grammar

Forms of writing

8

8.1 Which type of explanation?

Investigate different ways in which authors explain how the circulatory system works (or another topic if you prefer). How many different types of explanations can you find? What do you think about each type? Think about the writing as well as the illustrations. Which is most helpful? Why do you think that? Could any of them be improved? Look for explanations about other things. Are the same ways used to present the information? Do you think the best way of presenting information depends on what is being explained? Can you ever explain something without any writing? Do you all agree?

Different types of explanations have advantages and disadvantages. Written explanations are good for lots of fine detail. Labelled diagrams are good for showing different structures and how they fit together. Flow charts are good for showing the order in which things happen. Powerpoint is good for linking words and illustrations together. No single type of explanation is best for every type of information. People have different learning styles, so an explanation that suits one person may not suit everyone, and the age of the reader may make a difference. Sometimes explanations are created without words. However, it is difficult to ensure that the reader really understands without any text at all. Choose something that needs explaining and create different ways of presenting the explanations. Which do you think work well and why? Do your classmates make the same decisions?

8.2 Writing explanation texts

Talk about the purpose of an explanation text. Investigate the structure of the writing in some different explanation texts. Is there only one way to explain something or are there many ways? What tense do writers use? Do writers use their imagination? Which kinds of connectives do they use? Are your answers different for explanation texts for younger and older audiences? Look at some explanations in books and discuss why you think the authors chose to present them as they did. Would you structure the writing differently? Share your ideas. Do you all agree?

The title of an explanation text should be clear and unambiguous (a *how* or *why* title can be intriguing). The first paragraph should introduce the subject. The rest of the information should be written in logical steps, ending with a concluding paragraph. If you use technical vocabulary, think about including a glossary. Explanation texts are normally written in the present tense. Time connectives (like *then* or *next*) and connectives of cause and effect (like *because*, *so* and *therefore*) are helpful. There is no point in writing something that you don't understand. Accuracy is important, but that doesn't mean that you should just copy information. Now think of something that might need explaining e.g. *Why are successful athletes different shapes and sizes? How is spaghetti made?* Choose one of them and write your explanation. Try writing different versions for different audiences. What does another group think about your writing?

8.3 Illustrating explanation texts

Think about what sort of explanation might need an illustration. Investigate the illustrations in some explanation texts. What different kinds of illustration can you find? What is the difference between an illustration and a picture? Where might a graph or a map be useful? How do you decide the best way of illustrating the text? What does an illustration add to an explanation? Make a list of all the different forms of illustration that you find and share them with others in your class. Does everyone agree that they are illustrations?

Diagrams and illustrations should make your explanation clearer. They should help the reader to create mental pictures that would be difficult to create using just words. Sometimes words alone are sufficient, but on other occasions an illustration is necessary for a clear explanation. Illustrations can include graphs, maps, diagrams and pictures. How would you decide which to use in your explanation texts and when? Look in some books for explanations of things that you do not know about. Choose one that does not have any illustrations. Why do you think the author chose not to use illustrations? Could the author have included illustrations that would improve your understanding? Which sort would help the most? Do your classmates agree?

8.4 Non-chronological reports

Think about the purpose of a non-chronological report. Why do we read them? Investigate some non-chronological reports. How does dividing a report into sections or paragraphs help? Why might text boxes help? How do writers make it clear to the reader what each text box is about? Do they create some sort of order to the facts to make them clear to the reader? Is any technical vocabulary included? Do non-chronological reports only contain text, or do they include pictures and diagrams? Compare the features of several reports. What are their similarities and differences? Can you include opinions in a non-chronological report? What do your friends think?

The purpose of a report is to provide information about a topic. It differs from an explanation in that it doesn't usually attempt to explain how or why. It should start with a general introduction about the subject and continue with more detailed information, set out in paragraphs. Normally it is written in the present tense and the third person, using a formal style. Sub-headings help to group facts together and make it clear what each paragraph is about. Illustrations, diagrams, pictures and captions can help to clarify the ideas. You should select information from a range of resources, but try to avoid giving personal opinions in your report. Create a guide to the key features of writing a non-chronological report. Share it with others in your class. Does everyone agree?

8.5 Newspaper report

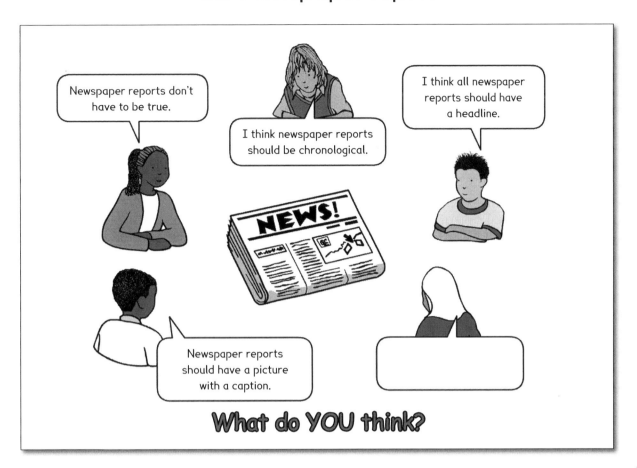

Look at a selection of newspaper reports. What do they have in common? What differences can you find? Are they all written in chronological order? Is chronology more important in some reports than others? What is the purpose of a headline? How long should it be? Is direct or reported speech used to provide quotes? Talk about the pictures and captions and what they add to the report. Look at a collection of reports about the same incident. Are there any differences? If a newspaper report is meant to be true, why are there differences when you read a report of the same event in different newspapers?

Newspaper reports are usually based on facts. Even so, reports of the same incident can vary, depending on who writes it and when it is written. (See 3.6 for more detail on bias.) Headlines should be short and snappy to catch the reader's attention. Alliteration and puns are often used. The opening paragraphs should answer all the Ws (who, what, where, when and why). Some of these should be expanded in the main body of the report. They don't have to be chronological. Pictures can be helpful, but are not essential. Now write your own report. Share this with other groups. How do they think it could be improved? Use your ideas to create a checklist for writing a good newspaper report. Does everyone agree with your ideas?

8.6 Sports report

Investigate some reports of football matches, athletics events and other sports. What information comes first? Are they in chronological order? What tense are they written in? Do they contain time connectives? Do the writers just describe the events, or do they give opinions too? What examples of this can you find? What are the differences between a sports report and other kinds of reports?

A sports report is a particular kind of non-fiction recount, in which the writer describes accurately what happened at a sports event. It normally starts with an opening paragraph that tells you when and where the event occurred and who was involved. Then what happened is usually presented in chronological order, with a closing statement at the end. It is written in the past tense, using time connectives. Some sports reporters use different styles. For example, they might open the report with a highlight from the event before writing the rest of the report. Different writers can give different interpretations of the same events. Although sports reports should give an accurate view of what happened, some readers enjoy reading the views of the reporters. Choose a sporting event and experiment with different writing styles to report it. Share your reports. Which do you think are the most effective? What features of your sports report are also features of a recount (for example, a grandparent's memories of starting school)? Create guidelines to help you write different recounts.

8.7 Diaries

Look at some examples of diaries. Is a diary always about things that have happened or can it be about things that are going to happen? What are the key features of an autobiography? How do these compare to a diary? If nothing special happens one day, do you think there should still be a diary entry? Talk to some people who write a diary regularly. How do they feel about letting someone else read it? Ask them to explain why they feel as they do.

A diary is usually a historical record for a person, but it can also be plans of future events. Most diaries are written in the first person and provide a record of significant events. They are usually written daily, but they don't have to be. Events are normally recorded in chronological order. They can include fact, opinion, feelings and emotions. The writer will often write as if speaking directly to the diary and exclamations are often used (*I've just had the worst day ever!*). Generally diary entries are written in the past tense, but they can be in the present or the future tense too. Because diaries are personal, diary writers often use a very personal style of writing. Sometimes writers use the form of a diary to write non-fiction stories. Write some imaginary diary entries for characters from the past and the present. Try to use different styles. Share them and discuss which are the most engaging and why.

8.8 Writing instructions

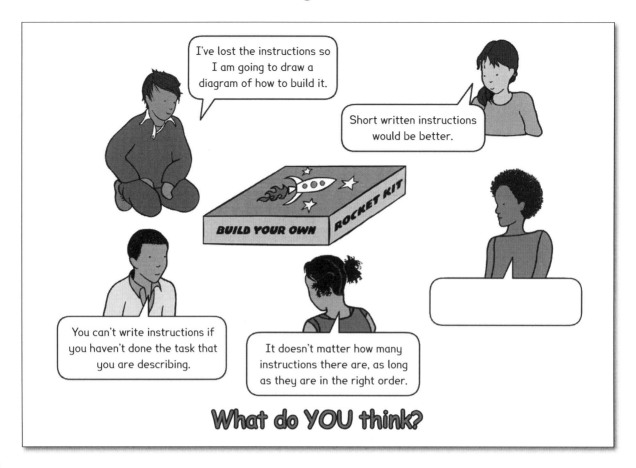

Look at some instructions. Read through them carefully, and either try them out or imagine yourself doing each step. What sorts of things are confusing and make you unsure of what to do next? How can the instructions be improved so that there isn't any confusion? What difference do you think it will make if the writer has done the task themselves first? Must instructions always be in the right order? How can a diagram help? Did you find examples of short instructions for doing something complicated? What did the writer do to keep them short?

Doing something yourself first usually helps you to write better instructions, although this isn't essential. Instructions should start with a goal or outcome (e.g. *how to bake a cake, how to put out a fire*). They should include a list of any items needed, numbered steps, time connectives and imperative (bossy) verbs. Short instructions tend to be easier to follow, especially for complicated tasks. Other possible additions are diagrams or pictures and top tips. Write some instructions for making something, such as how to make a paper boat or a kite. Get someone to follow them exactly. Discuss anything that might cause confusion and what would make them clearer.

8.9 Adjectives in instructions

Think about what you know about adjectives and when they are used. Investigate some instructions to see if you can find adjectives. Do they help to make instructions clearer or more confusing? Do they make things more interesting? Write some instructions for a simple recipe to go in a cookery book. Do not include adjectives. Now add some adjectives to your instructions. Do the adjectives make the instructions clearer or more confusing? What do your friends think?

Adjectives tell you more about nouns. They can describe many things, such as shape, size, colour, taste, cost or age. They can make stories more interesting and they can make instructions clearer, for example if you need to know what size tin to use to bake a cake, or what kind of glue to use when sticking things together. Instructions always include nouns and verbs, and frequently include adjectives and adverbs. All of these are important. Using adjectives is more important in some types of instructions than others. Create a style guide for when and how to use adjectives in writing.

8.10 Slogans

Look at a range of different slogans. How many of them are short? How many are funny? How many use alliteration? Do any have only a verb and a noun? Discuss with your group why the slogans you have found are effective. Which slogans do you always remember? Explain to the others in your group why you find them so memorable. Do they agree?

A slogan is a short, catchy, memorable phrase. For example, *Inspire a generation* was used as the slogan for the London Olympic Games in 2012. They are often used in advertising, where they become associated with a product or event, often with the addition of a catchy jingle. To be successful, they have to catch your attention. Slogans can catch your attention by alliteration, double meanings, humour, exaggeration, questions, logos and using jingles. Create some slogans of your own for a particular project or for something that is happening in your area or school, and share them with your friends. What do they think about your slogans? Can they suggest how the slogans might be improved?

Forms of writing

8.11 Being persuasive

Look at different forms of persuasive text. Are they all persuasive in the same way, or do the styles vary? Are images used to persuade? How do superlatives or comparatives help? Are there any rhetorical questions? Is any emotive language used? Are any other stylistic devices used to persuade readers? How is detailed information used? Look at your selection of persuasive texts. Which ones do you think are most effective and why? Do your friends agree?

Persuasive texts come in many different forms – advertisements, letters, debates, articles and reports. Their main purpose is to persuade the reader to see an argument from the writer's point of view. Persuasive writing usually includes the main arguments in a logical order, with evidence to support each point. However, too much information can be difficult to follow. The style of persuasive writing depends on the context and the audience. Images can be very effective in some contexts. In advertising, the writing and presentation are usually informal. The use of slogans, exaggeration, emotive language and repetition of key points can be very powerful in persuasion. Some people think it is unacceptable to use exaggeration to persuade someone to buy something. Why do you think that is? Now create some persuasive text of your own and share it with your classmates. What do they think about it and how it might be improved?

Forms of writing

8.12 Letters

Talk about why you might need to write a letter of complaint. Make a list of the things that you might complain about. Think about who it will be best to complain to in each case. What effect do you hope your letter will have? What sort of language will you use? If you are upset, should you show this by being rude? How else can you show how you were feeling? What effect will using lots of exclamation marks have? Why might writing a short letter be a good idea? Compare letters of complaint with other letters you might write. What are the similarities and differences between their structures and content?

A letter of complaint should be written using formal vocabulary. It should be polite but firm. Give as many details as possible but try to keep your letter short. If possible you should make it clear how you would like the problem resolved. Other letters normally have a similar structure and layout, although informal letters might not follow the usual letter-writing conventions. Write a letter complaining about the building of a block of flats in your local park, a letter to a local artist to ask if they will come into school to help with an arts project, and a letter to a friend who has moved to another town. What are the similarities and differences between the letters and why? How can they be improved?

Writing stories

9

9.1 Writing a story

Try writing a short story. What do you do? Do you write a plan first, or begin with the first line and just see where it goes? Does it make a difference if you have more time, or you are writing a longer story? Is it only longer stories that need a plan? Do you know the ending before you write anything? Discuss what you do with your friends. Do you all do the same things? Write a list of the pros and cons for different story writing methods used in your class.

Some people let the story emerge as they write, or start at the end and work backwards. However, lots of people find that it helps to have a plan before they start to write. There isn't one method that is best for everyone. There is a basic structure for a story that usually includes the opening, build-up, problem, resolution and conclusion. Generally, the opening sets the scene and introduces the main characters, the build-up creates the situation in which the problem occurs, the problem is where something goes wrong, the resolution solves the problem, and the conclusion rounds everything up. As you become more confident at writing stories you might give your story a different structure and surprise the reader by the way you write. Look at some short stories written by different authors. Try to identify the structures that they use. Choose one to use as the structure for writing your own story.

9.2 What is a good title?

Story writing competition today!

I am going to call my story Sam because it doesn't give the plot away.

That's not a good title. The title should always tell you the genre of the writing.

It's not a good title because it is not exciting enough.

I don't think you can choose your title until you have finished your writing.

What do YOU think?

Look at the titles of some books, not the front covers. Then decide which ones you would like to read and why. What do other people think? Are they interested in the same ones as you? Have you ever chosen a book because the title interested you and then found that you didn't enjoy it? Might some good books have poor titles? Is it better to think of the title before writing a story or to wait until it is finished? Should a title make it clear what the story is about, or should it keep you guessing? Choose a well-known story and think up some alternative titles for it. What do your friends think about them?

The title is an important part of a story. A creative or informative title can make a big difference to how readers react. Some people think that the best titles capture the feeling of a story, but not everybody agrees. Titles can be written in different ways. They can be a play on words (e.g. *You Only Live Twice*) or a popular expression (e.g. *Good as Gold*). They could be a line from the story, or refer to a character or place in the story. Look back at stories you and your classmates have written. Have you used any of these ideas? Try writing some alternative titles. Have you improved them?

9.3 Story openings

Compare the opening pages of stories by different authors. How many different kinds of story openings can you find? What other ways are there? Do similar types of stories use similar openings? Which ones make you want to read further? Make a list of all the different types of story openings you can think of. Which are your favourites? Why? What do you think a story opening should do?

Writers generally use four main ways of starting a story: a character, a setting, an action and dialogue. All of these can be effective starting points. When you are writing you need to decide whether to set the scene by describing a setting or character, or plunge the reader straight into the action. Sometimes writers start a story with a statement, a question or an exclamation. Some writers start with the ending, and the rest of the story shows the reader why the ending occurred. Choose a well-known story, such as Goldilocks and the Three Bears. Try writing it with different types of openings. What difference does it make to the story? Which do you prefer?

9.4 Story endings

Reread the final paragraphs of some of your favourite stories and look for different types of endings. Do the stories end with a character speaking, or a comment or observation by the author? Is everything explained or are there loose ends? Do any endings hint at what might happen next? Do certain types of stories always end in the same way? Which type of ending do you prefer? Why? Try rewriting a familiar story with a different type of ending. Add a sad ending or a cliff-hanger to a traditional fairy tale, or a happy ending to a sad story. What do your friends think of the new ending?

It doesn't matter what the story ending is, as long as it makes sense. There are many ways that writers end a story: a cliff-hanger, a twist or an unfinished ending. When you are writing a story you need to decide if an ending should resolve a problem or be a reflection on what has happened. You need to decide whether to have the ending reflecting life or whether to ensure that good triumphs over evil. There are plenty of examples of writers making each of these decisions. Some people say that they feel cheated by a trick ending to a story, such as *It was all a dream*. Why do you think authors sometimes leave some questions unanswered? Create a short story with an open and closed ending. Which do your friends prefer?

Writing stories

9.5 What part of a story is it?

Think about the statement and how it might be used in different stories. If the statement is a story trigger what might follow? If it is a cliff-hanger, where in the story would it be? If it is a story ending, what could have happened before? How would it resolve a story? Could it be a story ending and a cliff-hanger? When might it be simply a line of description? In which genres of writing could this sentence appear? Do you all agree? Write four paragraphs where you use the statement *And then the phone rang* in each of these ways. Compare them with others in your class. Do any of the paragraphs work better than others? Does the genre make a difference?

Writers use phrases like this to create different effects in their writing. The genre of the writing might influence which phrases they use and how. You need to see where the statement is in the text to decide what reaction a particular author hopes to get from the reader. You can use the statement *And then the phone rang* in lots of different ways in your writing, including all of those mentioned by the characters. Can you think of any other descriptive statements that can be used as story triggers, endings or cliff-hangers? Share them with your friends and see if they can use them in different ways. Are there any statements that can only be used in one way?

9.6 Creating a setting

Look at what your favourite authors do when describing a setting. Do they use any of the strategies mentioned? Which do you prefer? What about when you write a story? Do you prefer to set it in a familiar place, or would you rather use your imagination? Have you ever made up a setting based on a mixture of places you know? Was that easy or difficult? Have you ever written a story based in the future? Is that more challenging than writing in the present or the past? Why? Try writing short paragraphs using the strategies to create settings for a story. Share them with others in your class. What do they think about them?

There are no rules about the best way to describe a setting. It depends on the type of story that you are writing. However, when writers describe a setting they usually say something about the time and the place. If it is important they also say something about the social environment (e.g victorian England) and the physical environment (e.g. in the trenches during the war). The setting creates a mood for the story and provides the background for the plot. Are certain settings more suited to certain types of fiction? Collect examples of these and share what you find with each other.

Writing stories

9.7 Creating an impact

Look at some of your favourite stories. What is it about them that you really like? What do the writers do to create an impact? Do they all do it in the same way? Do they always include something to shock the reader? How do you think they decide what will shock? Do any of them write about different senses in a way that creates an impact? Does a 'larger than life character' feature in every story? Do any of them create an impact by using an unusual setting? Are there any other things that writers do to create an impact? What kind of writing has most impact for you and why? Does everyone have the same ideas?

You create an impact when you capture the reader's attention and make them want to read more. There are lots of different ways of doing this, including exciting events and interesting characters. What the subject is, who you are writing for, and the purpose of the writing are all things to consider when you decide how to create an impact. Different readers will respond differently to the ideas that you choose. Sometimes you might start writing, but then decide that you made the wrong decision about what kind of writing style to use to make an impact. It is alright to start again and change your writing style, if this is possible. Look at some stories that you have written. How could you change them to create more impact?

9.8 Understanding a story

Look at stories with and without illustrations. What difference do illustrations make to how well you understand the stories? How important is it to know how a character feels? What about stories where the action is not chronological? Are they easy to understand or confusing? Have you ever come across a word you don't know when you are reading a story? Does not knowing a word always prevent you from understanding the story? When might new words help? Compare a story that you found easy to understand with one that you found difficult. What are the similarities and differences?

Lots of different things can affect how well you understand a story. There isn't a single factor that is most important. Writers can't control some things, such as whether the reader can understand all the words. However, when you write you can help by trying to include words and ideas that are suitable for the particular age group. You can also think about whether to include illustrations, how the narrative is ordered and how much is revealed about characters or settings. Can you think of other features that will make a difference? Is writing a story that people understand the same as writing one that they enjoy? For example, if you use sentences and vocabulary that are very simple, will that make the story understandable but less enjoyable? Look at some of your favourite stories. Try to decide what makes them enjoyable as well as understandable.

9.9 Characterisation

Think about what it is that helps you to know a character in a story. Is it finding out what they look like, how they speak or what they do? Or do you need to know how they feel? Think about some of your favourite story characters. How did the author help you to know them? Write down a list of things you know about them, then look through the first few chapters to see how you learned these things. Make a note next to each personality trait or description to show what evidence you found.

Writers use different ways to make a character life-like. Sometimes they write about a character's external features, or how the character acts, or they describe events that happen. Sometimes they write about a character's internal thoughts and feelings, or how the character interacts with other characters. Sometimes they write about all of these. They may decide to reveal the character slowly to create a dramatic effect. There isn't a single best way – it depends on the circumstances. When you write a story you need to consider all possible aspects of your characters and decide which to use. Cut out a picture of an unknown person and create a personality for them. Decide what they are doing and why. What do they say? What are they thinking? Are they complex or even contradictory? Now build a story round the character. How could your story be improved?

9.10 Which senses to use

Look through some books and find some examples of writing that include describing using the senses. Think about how these descriptions make you feel and how they add to the picture that the writing creates in your mind. Think about some places you have been to. Was it always the sight of something that you noticed first, or was it the smell or the feel? Is any one sense more important than the others? Does it depend on the situation? Find a piece of writing that you have recently finished. Try rewriting part of it to include more reference to the senses. Does it make it better? Do your friends agree?

Most writers refer to the senses in their writing. This helps to develop the reader's understanding of the story. They do not always use all of the senses all the time. It would make descriptions too long. They choose which sense, or senses, to use to make the most impact. Sight is the sense used most frequently. Sometimes this is enough, but including other senses usually makes the writing better. Write a descriptive paragraph about somewhere you know. Start by only using the sense of sight in your writing. Now write the description again, but this time include all of the senses. Swap your writing with a partner, and look at how the addition of the other senses affects the images created in your mind.

9.11 Problems in stories

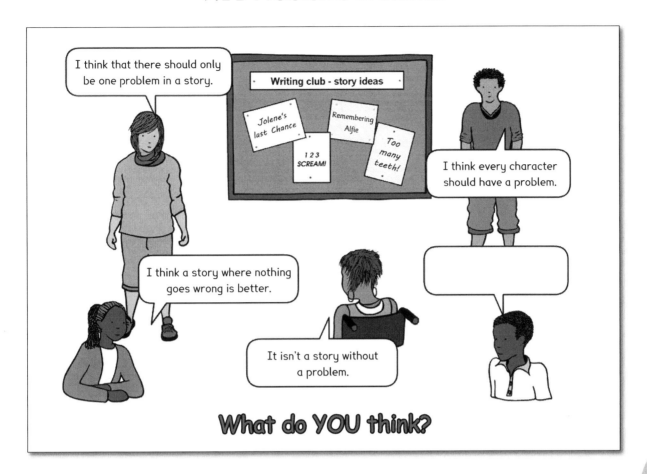

Talk to a friend about a story that you have both read. Was there a problem that the central character had to resolve? What was it? Did other characters have problems to deal with too? Think about other stories you have read. Have you ever read one where there wasn't a problem for the main character to face? Can you make a list of the types of problems that characters meet in stories you have read? What do you think makes a story interesting − is it the problem that the author presents, or is it how the character deals with the problem? Discuss this with your group. Do you all agree?

It is generally agreed that the stronger the problem in the story, the stronger the story. Most people would be bored by a story without a problem. Good stories often have several problems running in parallel. Authors make characters work hard to deal with problems or dilemmas in order to explore their personalities and show how they change and develop. The classic conflict is one person against another, such as between Jack and the giant in *Jack and the Beanstalk.* Conflict can also be against society or nature. Is it important that the problem in a story is resolved? Find examples of stories where the problem is resolved and where it isn't. Why do you think the authors dealt with the problems in the way that they did? What difference does this make?

9.12 Changing the plot

Think about the story of *Cinderella* and talk about what difference the changes suggested would make to the story. If Cinderella carries on dancing and the prince sees her in rags, would he change his opinion of her? If Cinderella's stepmother is kind to her, would Cinderella behave in a spoilt and selfish way like her stepsisters? If her fairy godmother gives her money, what might she do with it? Does the story need baddies in order for Cinderella to be a goodie? Write the ending to the story making one of the changes suggested. How has your ending changed the story? Do others think that your new ending is better or not? Why?

Cinderella has many of the features of a traditional fairy tale, such as the wicked stepmother and being granted wishes. Some of these features could change and it would still be a fairy tale. However, changing some features can change the type of story from a fairy tale to a mystery, a comedy, a disaster, and so on. It isn't possible to say in advance whether the story of *Cinderella* will improve if some of the events change. Choose a story type, such as a thriller. How would you change the story of *Cinderella* to that genre? Share your ideas with others in your class. What do they think and why?

Writing stories

Poetry, drama and playscripts

10

10.1 Poetry appreciation

Think about your favourite poem and tell someone else why you like it. Do they agree? Carry out a survey to find out which poem your friends choose as their favourite from a selection of different types. What reasons do they give? Does your class agree on a favourite type of poem? Nationwide competitions and surveys are frequently held to find out about people's favourite poem or poet. Look on the internet to find some results. Is one type of poem generally more popular than others? What reasons do people have for preferring different types of poems?

Different people like different poems. There are lots of reasons why we might like a poem. Perhaps it is because of the way it sounds or what it says, or maybe just because we know it well (perhaps by heart) and it is familiar. Some people have poems that they turn to at particular times for comfort, such as at a funeral, or on special occasions such as a wedding. Some poems are popular because they are an easy way to make people laugh, or they sum up strong feelings that many people share but find hard to express. Try writing a poem using the style of your favourite poem. How do people respond to your poem, and why?

10.2 Rhyming words

Find some different rhyming poems and nursery rhymes. Make a list of the rhyming words for each one. Talk about what it is that makes them sound the same or similar. Do all the rhyming words have the same number of syllables? See if you can find more words that rhyme with some of the words in each poem. Which words are hard to match? Share them with others in your class. What do they think about the rhymes you have created?

There are several different ways in which words can rhyme. Normally words that rhyme have the same or similar sounds at the end even if the letters look different, for example glow/toe/although. Sometimes more than one syllable sounds the same, such as middle and fiddle. Words can end in letters that look the same but do not always sound the same, for example lead and bead. These are often called eye rhymes. Lists of words that rhyme can be found in a rhyming dictionary. Some of the words that they list will be better rhymes than others. Choose a one-syllable word and take it in turns to find a word that rhymes with it. Score one point for a one-syllable rhyming word, two for a two-syllable rhyming word, and so on. Score two points for an eye rhyme. Who scores the most points? Keep a record of your ideas to use in your poems.

Poetry, drama and playscripts

10.3 Rhyme in poetry

Select a few poems from an anthology. Do they rhyme? Where are the rhyming words? What effect do they have? Are the rhymes always at the end of lines or are some in the middle of lines? Create a small collection of poems grouped by the way that they rhyme. What patterns can you find? Are there any that don't rhyme? Put these in a separate group. Do you like any of the types of poetry more than others? Why do you think this? Share your ideas. Do you all agree?

Poems can use several different types of rhyme. These include end rhymes (where the final words of lines rhyme), internal rhymes (where two words in the same line rhyme) and visual or eye rhymes (where the words look similar but sound different). Rhyme can be used in consecutive lines, alternate lines or more distant lines. Not all poetry uses rhyme. Some people say that rhyme was used to make poems easy to remember, before the printing press allowed them to be written down. Rhyming can narrow the choice of words and make poems predictable, but it can also make them memorable. Write a rhyming and non-rhyming poem. Does rhyming help when you are writing a poem or make it more difficult? Why? Would you choose a word just because it rhymed? What can you find out about the use of rhyme in other languages?

10.4 Repetition in poetry

Read aloud or listen to a poem, such as *There was an old woman who swallowed a fly*, that repeats a word or phrase. Is it easy to join in with, or does the repetition make it boring, or both of these? Which lines do you remember? Look through an anthology and find other poems that have repetition. Try reading them to each other. Why do you think the poet repeats certain words? Sometimes poets repeat sounds within words rather than the words themselves. Can you find an example of this? What effect is the poet trying to create? Try removing repeated lines from poems, or replace repeated words with a synonym. How does this affect your enjoyment of the poems?

Repetition of sounds is the basis for rhyme and alliteration. Repetition of key words, phrases, and sentence patterns can make you aware of the important themes and ideas in the poem. Repetition can also create rhythm, provide a structure for a poem and make a poem easy to remember. Sometimes repetition in a poem builds up the reader's expectation, so that you think you know what is coming next. When this expectation isn't met, it can create a sense of surprise and capture the reader's attention in a different way. Can you find an example of this? Write a poem that makes creative use of repetition. Share it with your group. Do they enjoy it? Why?

Poetry, drama and playscripts

10.5 How to write poetry

Look at some different kinds of poems and compare them. Try to work out if they follow any rules. If you find any rules, are they the same for each kind of poem? Are they the same rules as when you are writing a story or a report? Look for sentences in the poems. Are all of the poems written in correctly punctuated sentences? If a poem isn't written in sentences, how do you know how to read it? How does it make sense? Do you read poetry differently from prose? What happens if you punctuate a poem that doesn't have any punctuation? Try it. What difference does it make?

Poetry has many forms. Just as prose writing is governed by rules of grammar, most poetry also has rules about sequence, capitalisation, rhyme, rhythm and so on. Some types of poem have very precise rules about numbers of lines, words or syllables, rhyming patterns, and so on, for example haiku, limerick and sonnet. Some of these rules are very old. There do not appear to be any rules for free verse. Compare free verse with other types of poems and prose. How are they different? Work with your partner to create a poem about the rules for writing poetry.

10.6 Writing a play script

Find a play script to read. Look at both the dialogue and stage directions. Are these written in the same way? Are they written in Standard English? What punctuation has the writer used? Can you explain why? Which parts are written in the present tense? How is the play divided up? Does it have different scenes or acts? What other rules does the writer appear to have followed? Talk about what you have found out with other people in your class. Have you all reached the same conclusions?

There are rules for writing a play script. Normally it is written in the present tense and divided into scenes where different events occur. Speech marks are not used in dialogue, but other punctuation should be used accurately, so that the actor knows how to speak the line. There are other conventions, such as characters' names on the left followed by a colon, and starting a new line when a character starts to speak. Stage directions should be in brackets, use technical language (e.g. aside, stage right) and be in the present tense. Sometimes the characters might talk in slang or dialect. Find a few pages in a novel that contain dialogue and rewrite it as a play script applying the rules. What do you have to change or add so it makes sense to an audience? Try acting it out. How well does it work as a play script? How can you improve it?

Poetry, drama and playscripts

10.7 Role of the narrator

Think about plays that you know about that have a narrator. What does the narrator do? Talk to others in your class about the narrator's role. Do they take part in the action or comment on the action? Do they fill in gaps in the plot or tell you about things that happen off stage or before the play begins? Does the narrator give his or her own opinion about what the characters in the play do or say? Talk about the same plays and what they would be like without the narrator.

Not all plays need a narrator. Narrators are story-tellers that help to convey the action to the audience by speaking directly to them. This is sometimes called 'breaking the fourth wall'. They can offer background information, explain something or give their own point of view about what has been happening on stage. A narrator can be one of the play's characters that steps out of role briefly, or can be entirely separate from the other characters. In Ancient Greek plays the chorus acted as a narrator. Try writing a short play script with and without a narrator. Share it with others in your class. Which do you prefer and why?

10.8 Characters in a play

Think of some characters in a play you have seen. What do they look like and how do they behave? Talk to others in your class about your ideas. Have you ever seen the same play more than once? Were the characters the same or different? If you see the same play again and an actor wears a different costume, does it make a difference to what you think about the character? What if they change the way they move or the way that they speak? Who decides how an actor is dressed or moves on the stage, or what type of voice they use? If you have been in a play, what was it that helped you to feel most like the character?

Playwrights and directors create characters in several ways. What the actors wear, their movements and body language, how they speak and how they behave are all important. How they interact with the other actors is often the most important aspect of creating a character. You may see the same play more than once, and it will look and sound different each time because of the decisions made by the director. Find a scene from a play and decide how you would direct it. What will the actors wear? How will they speak? How will they move? What will they do when they are not speaking? Compare your decisions to those of another group. What do you think about each other's decisions?

132

10.9 Freeze frame

Choose one or two scenes from a play or story you know well and set up some freeze frames. Take it in turns to be in the freeze frame and ask the questions. Think about what you do and why. Talk about why freeze framing might be helpful. Can you explain what your character is thinking? Can others tell anything from your facial expression, the way you are standing and where you are in relation to the other characters? Can you answer questions as if you are the character? What is the difference between being in the freeze frame and asking the questions? Do you all agree?

Freeze framing is a good way of concentrating on a particular moment in a story. When the action is 'frozen', the people playing the different roles are able to focus on their character's feelings at that moment and why they might be behaving in the way they are. Being in the freeze frame is usually more helpful than asking the questions; generally being one of the characters makes you think more deeply about that character. Directors of films and plays use freeze framing when they are trying to get the actors to really understand the characters that they are playing. Watch a video extract of a play. If you are going to ask the actors to freeze frame, when would you ask them to do it and why? Share your ideas with others in your class. Do they agree?

10.10 Learning from hot seating

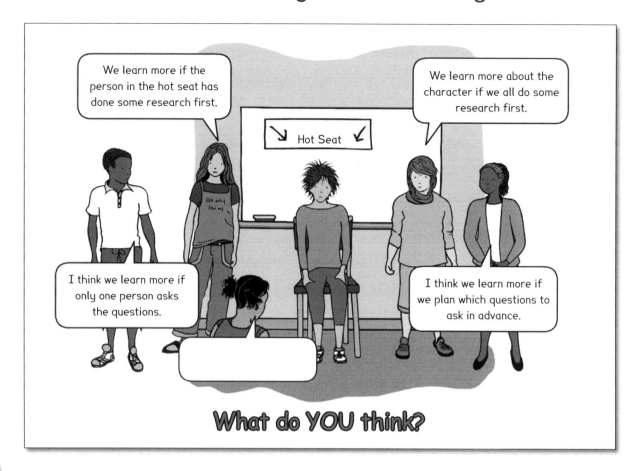

Shortly after your class has used hot seating, split into groups and talk about the experience and what you learnt. Talk about whether you think it is helpful for the hot seater to do some research first, or whether everybody needs to do some research first. Which questions are the most useful to ask? Are there any that could be planned in advance? What do you think would be the advantages and disadvantages of just one person asking the questions? Think about different ways of learning about characters. How is hot seating different from other ways of learning?

You can find out a lot of facts about a character in a book or from a website, but using hot seating gives you the chance to explore the character in more depth. You can ask your own questions, and you can also learn from the questions that other people ask. It is helpful if whoever is in the hot seat does some research in advance, but you can't necessarily plan all the questions in advance. The next time you hot seat make a recording and think about how you might improve what happens. How can you make sure everyone feels comfortable asking questions? What if you don't agree with the answer a person gives? What can you do to make sure you learn as much as possible using hot seating?

134

References:

Alexander R. (2006) *Towards dialogic teaching.* York: Dialogos.

Black, P., Harrison, C., Lee C., Marshall B. and Wiliam D. (2002) *Working inside the black box.* Kings College, London.

Black, P. and Wiliam, D. (1998) *Inside the black box.* Kings College, London.

Keogh, B. and Naylor, S. (1999) Concept cartoons, teaching and learning in science: an evaluation. *International Journal of Science Education,* 21 (4) 431-446.

Marshall, B. and Wiliam, D. (2006) *English inside the black box.* London, NferNelson.

Keogh, B., Dabell, J. and Naylor, S. (2008) *Active Assessment: thinking, learning and assessment in English.* Sandbach: Millgate House Publishers.

Wiliam, D. (2011) *Embedded formative assessment.* Bloomington, USA: Solution Tree Press.

Naylor, S. and Keogh, B. (2000) *Concept Cartoons in Science Education.* Sandbach: Millgate House Publishers.

Dabell, J., Keogh, B. and Naylor, S. (2008) *Concept Cartoons in Mathematics Education.* Sandbach: Millgate House Publishers.